. . . .

Crunch

I could hear the footstep just feet away from my tent. "That's just an animal Amber, you already knew you were going to hear things outside at night. It's probably just a raccoon or a deer," I told myself as I turned up the music on my phone to drown out some of the outside noise.

My dog Stevie and I had crawled into my tent around 6:30 that night because it was pitch black and I didn't want to be caught in the dark in the middle of nowhere. When I had pulled up to the campground in the middle of DeSoto National Forest in Mississippi that afternoon I was elated that I had the entire campground to myself. Now that the sun had set, that empty spot in the middle of the woods seemed more like a scene in a scary movie. So into the tent I went with my dog, a gun, bear spray, and a book.

Crunch

This footstep sounded bigger. "It's probably just a deer, chill out. Your dog isn't barking so it's nothing." I checked my phone. 8:30pm, no service, and 25% battery power left. 'That's okay,' I thought, "I came here to be alone anyway. I don't need my phone." Stevie was finally starting to fall asleep and I was getting close to being tired so I turned off my lantern and laid in the dark listening to more creatures walk around my tent. "Is that drums off in the distance? No, you're being crazy Amber, go to sleep." I started drifting off. Then the howls started. It was more of an eerie laughter off in the distance. Stevie looked up at me trying to figure out what the noise was.

Coyotes.

I smiled because I had never heard them before and this was one thing I knew for sure to expect. I wasn't even scared when they started yapping like I thought I would be. "See we can do this! Nothing to be afraid of!" I said to my goofy looking 8-month-old German Shepherd Lab mix I had rescued 4 months earlier.

But then I started to feel unsettled. I grabbed my phone to check the time and it the battery had finally run out. "What the actual fuck am I doing here??? I'm in the middle of nowhere by myself with a puppy that can't protect me. What if one of those coyotes smells my food and decides to come down to the campsite? Do I honestly think the thin lining of my tent is going to protect me from a predator???" I kept saying things like this to myself for at least ten minutes before finally grabbing the gun, bear spray, and Stevie and jumping into my car to sleep for the night.

Confused, Stevie slowly followed me to my tiny Volkswagen Beetle and hopped in the backseat. "We'll just sleep here tonight and I'll find us a better campsite tomorrow," I assured her. I started my car to charge my phone and let the heat run for a bit and that's when I saw the headlights come in. A white truck came flying into the campground. "That's got to be a ranger checking on the campsite," I said as I put the bear spray in my lap and watched the truck do a fast circle around the campground and come back my way. "They'll see me sitting in my car and stop just to let me know that the campground is clear and they are going back to the ranger station," I thought as the headlights crept into my car and nearly blinding me. It didn't stop. Instead, it flew right past me and back to the entrance of the campground. "That had to be a ranger."

I was still telling myself it was just a ranger when the truck turned off its headlights and parked near the entrance of the campground. "Maybe he's going to walk up here to tell me he was patrolling the campsite." I pulled the gun close to me while I looked off into the woods waiting for a man in uniform and a funny hat to start walking towards my car....

Nothing...

Minutes kept passing by then BANG! It was gunshots in the distance. I can't tell if they were coming from the truck or across the river but that was enough. No way was I going to stick around to find out.

"Fuck Fuck Fuck!" I kept yelling as my hands were shaking driving down the 5-mile dirt road that leads out of the campground. My phone still had no service. Who was I going to call anyway? The ranger station? The police? My grandparents? All of my stuff is back there. My tent, my new boots that are good for negative 15-degree weather, my hundred dollar sleeping bag I bought last minute because I realized the cheap one I bought would not keep me warm on a camping trip in the dead of winter. "What if they steal everything? At least you'll be alive, the stuff can be replaced. Forget the stuff, Amber." This conversation with myself continued 20 miles out of that damn National Forrest and to the closest hotel I could find.

As I checked into the hotel I kept telling myself it's okay to just turn back around and go back home in the morning. Did I really need to do this trip? What was I trying to prove to myself anyway? Camping in the middle of nowhere in the middle of winter was crazy. Obviously, this night has proven that it's too dangerous. I could have been murdered! What the fuck was I thinking? I'll go to bed with my oblivious dog in a warm hotel room that night and sleep on it.

When I drove to the campsite in the morning to get my stuff I called the ranger station to see if that could have been a ranger. A shocked southern woman on the other line said there were no rangers patrolling last night and then continued to lecture me for another 10 minutes about camping alone with no cell phone service and to make sure that I told someone where I was camping at all times and when I would return. She had no idea what I had planned on doing for the next month and I was not about to tell her.

Still shaking as I was pulling up to the campsite I saw my tent still there seemingly untouched. "What if I find a person sleeping in it? What if they stole everything inside?" I was almost too terrified of what I might find to unzip the damn thing. After sitting and hearing nothing for a few minutes I unzipped the tent, saw everything safe and sound and packed everything into my tiny car as quickly as I could. This was the moment of truth. Am I going to keep driving West and go through with this trip or am I going to turn back around and go home to Alabama? Every bit of common sense was telling me to go home and stop being ridiculous but there was another voice inside of me saying there was a reason I wanted to do this and I needed to remind myself why.

I couldn't go back to Alabama right now. Everything that I loved was there, but so was he. He was there and didn't want anything to do with me. None of my friends had room for my dog and I, my family said I could stay with them but I'd have to do something with my dog. I wasn't going to get rid of Stevie or put her in a shelter while I figured life out. I had no home to go to except the tent in my car and the ground that we set it up on. I had to keep going.

So I grabbed my dog, got in the car, typed 'Texas' into my GPS and we drove as fast as we could away from that place.

SEPTEMBER 25, 2018

Rosyln- Bon Iver

Dear Me,

This break up sucks. It sucks so bad for a million reasons, but it will not break you. I know you've been let down a lot of times in your life and when you met this one you thought he was finally your something good. Well… he was. But sometimes the good things don't last forever. Sometimes good things come into our life for a short period of time to teach us something about our self and then they leave before they become something bad. You have been given a gift with this breakup. Pretty soon he will still be something good in your memory without all of the bad.

When you start to get mad and miss him think about all the good things that came out of that relationship. You learned so much about yourself and your capacity to love. You know who you are and what you truly want in life. There was a gift in that. He may not be the one that gives you what you want in life but he was the one that showed you what you want. It's okay to miss him and be sad but don't try to trap him. That is not love. Move on. Let him be free and love him the best way that you can from a distance.

It will be okay.

Love,

Your Soul

OCTOBER 2, 2018

Coming Down - Bon Iver

Dear Boss,

I am going through the hardest breakup I have ever gone through and I think it is because of another girl. I'm trying really hard to not let it affect my job but I'm really struggling to keep it together right now. I can't eat, I can't sleep, and I can't stop crying.

I'm going to take the rest of the week off to drive home and clear my head for a few days. I don't know what else to do but I have to get through this.

Thank you for understanding,

Alabama

OCTOBER 3, 2018

I'll Be Good - Jaymes Young

Dear God,

I know we haven't talked in a while, but I know you are showing me something big right now. Thank you for helping me keep it together on the phone with him today when he finally told me the truth about her.

I really thought I would scream and cry or beg him to pick me instead. But you came through me and showed me that if I truly do love him I have to let him go be with her and if they are meant to be I cannot change that. If he is meant to be with me he HAS to do this to figure it out.

For the first time in my life, I actually am handing this over to you. I never in a million years thought I could love someone so purely that I can let them go and be okay with it. But God *please* show me what it is you are trying to show me. This hurts so much to just walk away and I really need you right now. If he is meant to come back to me please just give me a sign. I feel so lost right now. I don't know how I'll handle it if he really does end up with her forever. Please help me find the strength to be happy for them and move on.

Devastated,

Amber

OCTOBER 4, 2018

Angela - The Lumineers

Dear Angie,

Thank you for letting me and Stevie come stay with you for a few days. I know it's not like our typical hangouts because I'm so sad, but being around you really has been good for my soul right now. I appreciate that I can always be myself around you no matter what.

Sorry I cried over my french toast at Big Bad Breakfast this morning. It was just the first real meal I'd eaten in three days and who knew that I could be so happy over being able to finally eat again that I would actually burst into tears in public? I'm sure I looked like a crazy person but who cares!

I know my puppy is like having a toddler in the house and I'm sorry that she ate all of your cat food. She loved playing in your backyard though and it's nice to have her out in nature instead of in the city for a while.

I know I've been unusually quiet this trip home, it's just so hard to get all of my words out. I think you can hear my heart and don't need me to speak though. That is one of the things I love about you. It's amazing the bond we have after being best friends for almost thirty years. (OMG it's almost thirty years!)

I love and appreciate you more than you know.

Amber

PS. You are not allowed to get me stoned for a while! I thought it would help but instead it just made me feel the pain of the breakup even more! That was WAY too intense! I've never been a good pot smoker. It doesn't agree with me at all!

OCTOBER 6, 2018

. . . .

Possibility - Lykke Li

Dear Hanna,

Thank you for answering all of my crazy calls this past week and listening to all of my rants and raves about boys and this shitty breakup. I know I promised I wouldn't cry in front of you while we were hanging out today but all of a sudden everything just hit me like a ton of bricks and I couldn't stop myself.

Driving backroads around town with you did make me feel better though. Thanks for letting me crash in your room while you went out with your friends. I don't know why sleepovers with you always seem to help my soul but they do. I think it's because it reminds me of when I was a teenager and I can let go of all my adult problems for a second. Plus it reminds me when you were a small kid and you just used to make me laugh so hard at the random things you would say. You still do that now.

You are wise beyond your years kid and I love you so much. You have the whole world in front of you and I cannot wait to see where this life takes you. Don't ever let a boy change you to fit his mold. You are so unique and it would break my heart to see the light inside of you go dim.

You're also the only person in the world I'd let drag me to church this weekend and make me watch the Demi Lovato documentary. You're the best little cousin and friend I could have ever asked for.

Love,

'Mom'

OCTOBER 8, 2018

Good Kisser - Lake Street Dive

Dear J,

I'm so mad today. It must have been the shock that's kept me from being angry for the past two weeks but today it finally hit me.

If you really loved me and never meant to hurt me like you said then why would you even lie to me about her in the first place? That alone speaks volumes. The worst part is you kept making jokes about me having another boyfriend when in reality I cut every other guy out of my life because I was so dedicated to you.

You said you don't want me to feel like I'm not good or pretty enough for you, but it's too late. How can I compete with your high school girlfriend who was always the prettiest and most popular girl in school and I was just the tomboy that no one ever noticed… including you. I knew it was too good to be true that you finally saw me the way I saw myself. You never truly did see the real me our whole lives. Was I just used as a place holder until she came back into your life?

My heart feels like it was completely ripped out of my chest. I've cried every day for two weeks, but not today. I refuse to cry for you today. Today I will be angry and try to forget how much I love you.

I'll forget all the flights we took to see each other. I'll forget how excited we would get when we talked about you moving to Chicago before having a sudden change of heart. I'll forget the countless hours on the phone of you saying how much you loved me, how we were teammates and how you would never hurt me. I'll forget that when I adopted Stevie she was supposed to be 'our' dog. I'll forget the road trip we took across the country and falling in love with you while we were camping in Yosemite. I'll forget every little nice thing you ever did for me because I know that when I wasn't around you were doing the same things for her.

Instead, I'll remember how you blindsided me with the break up then ghosted me when I asked you why. I'll remember that you broke up with me over text because you were too coward to do it in person. I'll remember when you started nitpicking everything about me like my taste in music or how I was a cat lady that liked to knit and how I didn't fit into your list of 'the perfect girl.' It all makes sense now because that's probably the same time you started seeing her again.

Eventually, I will move on and stop loving you. One day I will realize that I am the better woman and you made the wrong choice. One day you will realize that too and by then I will have finally stopped feeling so broken over you.

That's the worst part of this all. For some crazy reason, I still love you and part of me is hoping that you'll get her out of your system and come back to me. How sick is that? All I want to do is hate you and I can't.

I hope you are happy with this choice.

Like we always said,
"'I see you."

Amber

OCTOBER 10, 2018

Landslide - Fleetwood Mac

Dear J,

I took Stevie to the water for the first time tonight. We snuck down to the beach by my apartment after it closed and I let her run around in Lake Michigan. She LOVED it. She kept jumping at the waves and trying to bite the water and it was one of the funniest things I've ever seen her do.

I wanted to text you about it because we kept wondering how she would like the water when I first adopted her. You'd have loved to see how excited she got over it.

I'm trying my hardest not to text you now and every other time that I miss you.

I still hate going to the dog park by my place because it reminds me of you. It doesn't feel right going there without you to throw frisbee with Stevie and I. We both miss you.

This sucks.

Amber

OCTOBER 11, 2018

Musta Been Something - Lake Street Dive

Dear Diary,

I keep going over and over in my mind the things I should have done differently with him. I wish I would have played guitar with him instead of feeling too intimidated by him to let him hear me sing. He was just so talented and I didn't want to fumble over chords in front of him. I don't think he would have thought I was good enough anyway. But now I wish I would have. I played all day today and it felt so good. I want to keep playing and singing. That's been my passion since I was a little kid but I let my fear hold me back from doing what I love to do.

I also wish I wouldn't have gotten frustrated with him over the little things. Maybe if I kept my cool more often I wouldn't have pushed him away. Or if I played more hard to get. I think I freaked him out when we'd talk about him moving to Chicago and I was so gung-ho about it. I just got so swept away in our love affair. He wrote me a song and it was just all over from there... damn musicians! I wish I would have sent him the song I wrote about him. He kept saying he didn't know how to be what I needed. I should have listened and backed off some. I should have just let him be.

I wish I didn't tell him about my wild past. I don't think he realized that I was trying to show him that when we started dating everyone else fell away from my world and he was the only man I saw. Him seeing my soul the way that I thought he did meant more to me than any other man looking at me ever could. I feel absolutely sick at the thought of ever getting intimate with anyone else again after him. Then I think about him getting intimate with her and I feel dead inside. I gave him all of me and I feel like I can never get that back.

I wish I didn't fall asleep during his favorite movie when we watched it. I could tell that disappointed him. I wish I lived closer to him. The distance was so hard on both of us.

I wish I wouldn't have cried so much to him about my problems. I should have listened more and talked less.

I know I've been in a pity party the past two weeks, but in all reality, I'm probably not the greatest girlfriend in the world either. I stopped doing things that I loved and became too consumed with our relationship. I wish I would have kept a better balance with life and took better care of myself while we dated.

Anyway, hindsight is your heart telling your mind, "I told you so," right?

If I ever do fall in love again (and that's a big if) I'll do it differently. I wish I didn't think about him so much. At least the pain

is turning into numbness and I can finally eat and sleep again....
My therapist would call that progress. There's part of me that's
afraid to get over the pain because that means he's really gone.
Losing him is the hardest part of it all.

I'm rambling now and I should go walk Stevie.

Until next time...

Me.

OCTOBER 12, 2018

The House That Built Me - Miranda Lambert

Dear Meemaw,

I know you are mad that I am thinking about moving back home even after he broke my heart. I understand that you are worried that I'm ruining my career and my life, but trust me when I say that I am not.

Remember thirteen years ago when I moved to California because I was heartbroken over a boy and you thought it was a bad idea? It ended up being the best decision of my life. Look at all the places I have traveled and the amazing jobs that I have had during my career!

Somehow I landed a job in the third largest city in America and a billboard with my face on it! How crazy is that?!? I've met a lot of my idols (and a lot of your idols), made a lot of money and did every single thing that I set out to do. You were so terrified that I was being reckless when I set out to do all these things and worried that I wouldn't make it. Well, I did! And you were proud.

But here is the biggest lesson that I've learned during all of my travels: No amount of money or fame in the world can truly make you happy. It can make you comfortable but it's really just keeping me numb from the pain of not having what I really want in life. Money and fame are like morphine for the wounded soul. It eases the pain for a little while, but it doesn't actually heal the wound.

The root of my pain isn't being poor or unknown. The root of my problems has always been love. Not knowing how to love myself, loving the wrong people, searching for love in all the wrong places and running away from the people that love me the most.

I'm so tired of hurting Meemaw. Coming home is coming back to all the people that I know and love. The people who know the real me before I became 'Alabama' with a lot of money and a huge following. The people who know and love Amber.

What's the point in having all that other stuff with no one to share it with? I want to be able to come visit you whenever I want or go to the movies with Hanna on a random Tuesday night or go fishing with Peepaw before he can't fish anymore or sit with Nanny and watch Oprah before she gets sick of watching TV with us. I want to have friends and family over for dinner whenever I want. I want to belong to a community.

Meemaw I love you and I know you are worried about me but don't be afraid for me. Be happy because I will finally be happy too.

Love,

Amber

OCTOBER 12, 2018

Vice - Miranda Lambert

Dear Cigarettes,

You are so bad! I started smoking you again and I'm so mad at myself for it. I was doing so great without you. I had quit you, started going to the gym and was taking such good care of myself. Then something bad happens and here I am, a week into being a smoker again.

The irony is how much I hated that he smoked because I knew that it was slowly killing him. It made my apartment smell awful when he came to visit. I'd get angry when he'd leave me at restaurants to go outside and smoke. I'd get frustrated when he wanted to smoke in my car. But here I am doing the same shit and I feel like I can't quit. I know you are bad for me. I smell bad, I can't breathe, you're a waste of my money and I feel like absolute shit.

But the thing is you are soooooo good. When I feel like I can't handle the sadness of him leaving me you give me a moment of relief. When the world feels like it's closing in on me I can take a break and put in my headphones and take a long slow drag of you and feel like everything will be okay.

Plus you're distracting me from wanting to drink too much and I'm proud of myself for that. God knows if I get drunk I'll text him and I can't do that to myself. If I text him I know he won't respond or if he does it will just hurt me more and I don't want him to know how much I really am hurting. I don't want him to know that some days it feels like I'm barely holding on. I want him to think I'm out being the girl that he fell in love with. I want him to think I am happy without him. I want him to be the first one to reach out because he actually misses me and not because he thinks he has to. I don't want to guilt him into loving me again.

Ugh, I just want to quit you and be done with this shit.

Angry consumer,

Amber

OCTOBER 13, 2019

Guaranteed - Eddie Vedder

Dear Angie,

Ignore my drunk FaceTime last night about doing my own version of *Into The Wild*. I had a few beers and was watching the movie (which is one of my favorites and you still need to see it yourself!) and after four beers doing this myself seemed like a great idea! I mean Meemaw doesn't want me to move back to Alabama, he doesn't want to see me or even know that I asked my job to let me move back home the morning before he broke up with me. I honestly don't know where home feels like to me either.

But this morning after sobering up a little and sleeping it off I woke up thinking that it's crazy for me to try to do some sort of *Into The Wild* trip. My job is about to let me out of my contract and I'm going to need to save all the money I have and figure out what the hell I'm going to do with my life instead of roaming across the damn country getting lost and blowing what I have on gas and campsites. I do appreciate you offering to watch my cats though! You really are my best friend and I appreciate you for supporting even my craziest of ideas! Next time I call you with an idea like that though please just tell me I'm crazy and don't let me come up with such wild ideas!

Love,

Amber

The Gold - Manchester Orchestra

Dear J,

I'm so mad at you. I'm even angrier at myself for wanting to talk to you. It's all I can do to keep from texting you tonight. I've typed out three messages already and then deleted them all.

I miss you so much, and I can't even say hello to the person I thought was my best friend. I think that's why I'm angry at you the most.

'I see you.'

Amber

OCTOBER 17, 2018

· ·

Dream - Bishop Briggs

Dear J,

I had a dream about you last night. I don't remember all of it but we were having a conversation. I do remember in the dream you said if I want you to come back to me that I had to leave you alone. And there was a fireplace in the dream if that's supposed to mean anything?

I'm trying to leave you alone and not reach out to you, but sometimes it is so damn hard. I wonder if you dream about me too. It sounds crazy but it feels like I was actually talking to you last night. I know this is weird but I had a dream that I had a conversation with her too before I even knew what was happening with you both. The night before you broke up with me, I had a dream that you were camping with her and I caught you in a lie about it. Then it came true. (At least the part about the lie, I don't know about camping and I don't want to know honestly)

The thing is I think I knew this was going to happen when we started dating but I told myself I was crazy and ignored that gut feeling. I knew when you started lying to me about her but I ignored it. I wish now that I would have just spoken up and worked through it.

Sometimes I tell myself to move on because you don't love me, you love her. But other times I think deep down you do love me and just think you're not good enough for me and she was the easier choice for you. My gut won't tell me the true answer to that one. Maybe I'm not ready to know yet. Either way it was good seeing you last night even if it was a dream.

I miss you,

Amber

OCTOBER 18, 2019

. . . .

The Wolf - Eddie Vedder

Dear Angie,

I know I said my trip was crazy and I changed my mind after sleeping on it, but honestly... the more I think about it, the more it makes sense. I started buying all of these things I'll need for survival out there. I love to camp. I don't know when I'll ever get a chance to just travel for a month on my own ever again. No one really wants me to come back home either. Why NOT do my own version of *Into the Wild*?

I just want to get lost in nature and not have to worry about all of the other bullshit going on in my life right now.

I can go out there with Stevie, focus on being in the moment. Spend time with her and myself and figure out a way to get over him. I can really sit and figure out what I want to do with my life instead of the same old thing I've been doing for years that obviously isn't making me happy. And who cares if it's in the dead of winter! I'll stay south and go to all of the warm places and get to skip the damn Chicago winter this year!

Sooo.... if the offer still stands to watch my cats would you please do it for a month while I go figure life out? Thank you!

I love you,

Amber

OCTOBER 19, 2018

. . . .

Space - Maren Morris

Dear guy who sat next to me on the plane,

You have no idea how important it was to sit by you today! I believe the universe sends signs to us all the time to help push us in the right direction and you were definitely a sign. You don't know the extent of the trip I've been planning to go into the wild, but I can say it's all I've been able to think about for the past two weeks and I've been almost obsessed with it.

Doing something like this alone feels crazy and topping it off with the fact that I might not have a job soon honestly scares the shit out of me. But then I sat by you. We talked about the outdoors and I found out you work for a company that sells camping and outdoor gear was sign enough for me. Then you gave me a friends and family discount to get more gear and I knew that was God yelling in my face 'Here's a resource to buy the rest of the things you need, DO THIS.'

Our conversation also took my mind off of the real reason I was flying home today. It was supposed to be my 15-year high school reunion and he was supposed to go with me since we graduated together. This was going to be the first time we went somewhere that people we grew up with would know we were a couple. But now we are broken up and Thank God the reunion was canceled, but this trip home just reminds me of him and how he doesn't want to see me and that he's with her.

Anyway, I'm using the coupon you gave me to buy boots that are good in negative 15-degree weather and warm clothes for my trip. I was going to skimp on those things for a cheaper option but now I don't have to and I won't freeze to death if it gets too cold out there! You may have literally saved my life on this trip!

Thank you for that. I hope you enjoy your first rock climbing trip in Alabama.

Cheers,

The chatty girl on the plane

OCTOBER 20, 2018

Sick Cycle Carousel - Lifehouse

Dear Cody,

I'm sorry that I hurt your feelings by pushing you away when you tried to kiss me last night but I told you already not to flirt with me. I did at one point in my life love you but you have to understand that right now there's no way I can even think about loving you. I can't even imagine the thought of ever loving anyone else ever again. The wound is just too fresh. If I'd have kissed you I'd have wished you were him and I'd get sad all over again.

Maybe this is my karma for how badly I broke your heart a few years ago. He did almost the exact same thing to me that I did to you and God does it hurt. I had no idea that love could hurt so bad. But you have to believe me that when I did that to you a few years ago I didn't feel great about it either. I just knew that in the long run, I couldn't love you the way that you needed me to move you. Maybe that's how he feels about me too.

I don't know why I feel this way about you and sometimes I wish I could love you because I know how much you do love me but I just can't. I will always be fond of you as a friend but that is it.

I hope one day you find a girl that's made just for you but it won't be me. My heart belongs to someone else and trying to be with you wouldn't be fair because I wouldn't mean it. I can't force my heart to want something that it just doesn't want. And unfortunately, I can't make it stop wanting something that it wants even if that something doesn't want me back. I hope you can understand.

Amber

OCTOBER 23, 2018

Smile Lines - Incubus

Dear High School,

You really sucked! I mean don't get me wrong you were a lot of fun too, but you were so hard to survive. For girls like me, it was always hard to fit in. I was different and awkward. I didn't really know how to talk to people and when I finally did figure out how to make friends the anxiety at times would feel paralyzing. The one thing I was good at was the school part but being a nerd in high school isn't exactly fun either. Not to mention average girls like me were rarely even noticed. I didn't have boys beating down the door to take me to homecoming or prom. I actually had to break down and finally ask a friend to go with me to prom my junior year because I didn't have a date to go with me.

Even the guy I fell in love with now that we are adults never noticed me in high school. He never saw me the way I saw him our entire childhood. I had a crush on him for so long but to him, I was just one of the guys that hung out in the same group while he dated all these other beautiful girls. The girls that I grew up wishing that I looked like. No wonder it felt too good to be true when he actually noticed me and we started dating fifteen years later. Of course, he was going to end up leaving me for his high school girlfriend. The girl who was always on the homecoming court or nominated for prom queen. The beautiful girl that I always wished I looked like but never did.

The even funnier part of this all is that here I am fifteen years later thinking I had outgrown my awkward high school phase. I got out of our small town drama. I became a successful person. I didn't become the typically beautiful person everyone noticed but I feel beautiful in my own right. I was confident and happy. I became bigger than all the insecurities that come from being an awkward nerdy girl in high school that no one noticed. So how in the world am I sitting here weeping over some silly boy from back home who can't even stop reliving his old small town cycle from the past? I feel like an idiot even saying this out loud. It's hysterical even. When I take my emotions out of it and look at the whole picture I can't stop laughing at myself and how ridiculous this all really is. How did I let myself fall into this dumb situation? I feel like I've gone backward fifteen years and all of a sudden I'm the seventeen-year-old awkward me again letting this boy who will never change have all this power over me when really I'm the one he should be sad over losing.

High school really doesn't end, does it? I still feel like the outsider. Unseen and not fully accepted into the popular crowd. Isn't it ironic that even my job is like being in high school? Trying to fit in with the 'in' crowd in Nashville. The people who actually have an influence in the music industry but treat it like a club that only the exclusive can have access to. Or even trying to make listeners fall in love with me on the radio. It's all a popularity game. I got into talking on the radio because of my passion for music but really it's just an adult version of high school all over again. We think as adults we change and grow up but we are really the same. Just with more money and no parents to scold us every time we mess up.

I wish I had a time machine. If I did I'd go back to sixteen-year-old me and say this:

"Don't take yourself so seriously. Yes, you will do embarrassing things that you're not proud of, but so will everyone else. Sing. If you love to do it who cares what everyone else thinks. Ten years from now you won't remember half of these people and they won't remember you either so sing. Sing loudly."

"Enjoy living at home because taking care of yourself and doing your own laundry sucks no matter how old you are. Don't stress yourself too much over a broken heart, in a few years you will change and be glad you didn't end up with the boys that hurt you. Take more pictures, even if you are ready to get out of here you're going to miss this place in a few years and wish you could go back. Don't rush to grow up. Everything will change but at the same time nothing really changes at all and one day you'll look in the mirror and wonder where all that time has gone and you'll realize you spent most of it worrying about the future instead of living in the present."

Anyway, here we are fifteen years later and high school never really ended, did it? At least not for me in this particular moment and the irony is not lost on me. High school you really sucked.

Sincerely,

Your 2003 Class Clown - Amber Cole

OCTOBER 27, 2018

Boxcar - Shovels and Rope

Dear Therapist,

Remember when I came back from Alabama in May and we talked about how it was a bad idea for me to date J? I had a bad habit of dating guys from back home and stringing them along for a few months then breaking their hearts and moving on to the next. Remember when I broke down crying because I didn't want to do that to J? So you and I agreed that I would stay away from him and work on myself.

Well… I lied. I did date him and I wanted to enjoy every moment of it without over analyzing it in your office once a week. I was so proud of myself because this time I was different. I gave it an earnest try and I actually fell completely in love with him. I stopped looking for attention from all the other guys in my life. He was different from the ones before. I wasn't going to break his heart like all the others. I actually fell in love with him.

Except for this time, he was the one who broke my heart. How ironic is that? Actually, you'd probably tell me it's not ironic at all that somehow I sabotaged this myself by dating a guy I knew was emotionally unavailable.

I got a dose of my own medicine and man is it bitter. You'd be proud of how calmly I handled the breakup when he finally told me about the other girl though. I didn't cry or beg him to stay even though I wanted to. That's progress, right?

But tonight a mutual friend of ours posted a video of him with her singing together and it crushed me. All of my insecurities came flooding back. Why would he never play guitar like that with me when he knew I loved music just as much as he did? I know I'll be fine but just seeing it tonight feels like my heart is sinking into my stomach and I wonder if I'll ever get over this.

I'm quitting our sessions from now on. I appreciate how much you've helped me grow over the past year but it is time for me to stop talking and start using what I've learned from you in the real world. Plus I'm planning a big change soon and I can already hear you saying it's going to be a bad idea. Truthfully I'm worried if I tell you about what I want to do you'll talk me out of it and I can't let that happen.

I'm sure this isn't the last you'll hear from me so I'll just say, "Goodbye for now."

Amber

OCTOBER 31, 2018

Halloween - Walker Hayes

Dear Halloween,

You are typically my favorite holiday of the year but I just can't celebrate this year. It feels weird walking around the city this afternoon seeing everyone happy and dressed up while I feel like a ghost in limbo. This is the time I want to be around loved ones but everyone I care about is in Alabama. I wished he was here to see the beautiful fall colors in the city. When the trees change it's the most spectacular blend of yellows, oranges and reds mixed into the skyline. It feels like magic in Chicago this time of year but for some reason the magic is just flowing all around me but avoiding me. I'm so tired of being sad. This isn't me. I hate being numb to the world moving around me.

I want to join the party so bad but I just feel like an outsider looking in and trying to figure out a way to belong to something. Anything. I feel like I've been wearing so many different masks for so long, pretending to be who I needed to be for whatever person I was with at the time that I can't find the real me anymore. It's like I keep peeling away layers of mask after mask and I can never get to *my* face. The masks never end. Maybe that is my costume this year. I am everyone that I've ever pretended to be yet I am nobody.

Sincerely,

Amber

. . . .

Sometimes it's a Bitch - Stevie Nicks

Dear Stevie,

I know you're a little confused about what's going on today but we had to get your surgery to take out the tennis ball you stole at the dog park and swallowed. I still can't even believe you managed to get that down your throat even if it was a mini version of a damn tennis ball.

I was so scared it was going to get stuck in your throat and you wouldn't be able to breathe. DON'T EVER DO THAT AGAIN. I looked like a crazy person at the dog park dragging you home while frantically calling the vet to make sure you weren't going to die over a damn tennis ball!

Speaking of the vet, I know they love you! We need to get your surgeon and vet techs a Christmas present this year. Especially since they took the time to put a photo of your namesake (Stevie Nicks) on your bag of medicine we had to take home. I'm going to frame that alongside your x-ray of that disgusting ball! I can't believe they actually gave that nasty thing back to us after taking it out of your belly. That tennis ball and every other toy small enough for you to swallow is going in the trash tonight!

I know the cone sucks, but you did this to yourself and now you need to heal properly! Please stop trying to run and jump that's not allowed for another two weeks and we really can't afford any more surgeries right now. Especially if we are going to do the trip I'm planning for us in a few months. I can't afford another $1400!!!! I love you though and I am really happy you are okay even though I ask myself all the time if I'm really ready to take on the responsibility of a puppy right now. Please don't swallow anything life-threatening while we are out in the wild!

Love,

Mom

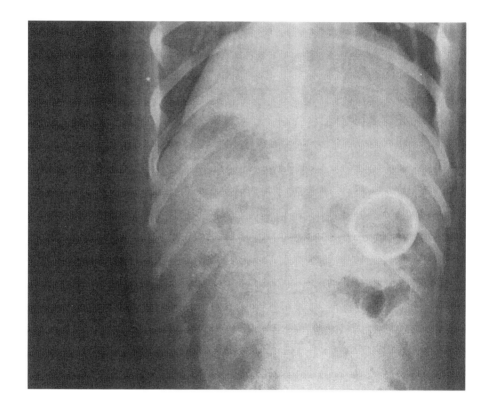

NOVEMBER 4, 2018

Love of My Life - Queen

Dear J,

I have wondered how long it would take you to reach out to me after we broke up. Sometimes I thought it would be only days. Then as time went on I told myself maybe you'd reach out in a month. I had finally started accepting the fact that it might never happen and I was actually okay with that... Then you reached out to me today. Six weeks was how long it took.

How perfect your timing was! I was finally starting to feel excited about being single again and feeling good about myself and the fact that I could move on and be free but then a few simple words over a text message sent me spiraling back into sadness over you. "How are you and Stevie? Good, I hope" had me bursting into tears in the middle of the movie theatre watching Bohemian Rhapsody.

I don't know why I even started crying. Hearing from you is all I've wanted for the past six weeks so why am I not happy? I want to respond but what do I even say? "I'm picking up the pieces of my heart that you shattered." or "Stevie has forgotten you and I'm sad about that because she loved you and I know how much you loved her." Or "You're missing Stevie grow up faster than I thought she would and sometimes I hate you because I adopted her thinking she was going to be our dog and raising her alone is so overwhelming." or should I keep it upbeat with "Stevie is wonderful and everyone we pass on the street loves her and she's becoming an even better dog that we thought she would be." Or how about the truth, "I miss you every single day and my life is about to drastically change and I'm terrified."

I can't say any of that to you. I'm scared to even respond because I don't want to give myself false hope that you could want me back when there is no hope. I can't go through this pain anymore. I was so crushed and confused when I heard those words come from your mouth after I was so sure you'd be the last person in the world who could ever hurt me the way you did. I do still love you and miss you but right now I can't even speak to you.

Amber

NOVEMBER 6, 2018

You're Somebody Else - Flora Cash

Dear Me,

I know you're freaking out right now, but remember this: When you leap a net will appear. This is the day you've been waiting for and now you finally know you are about to be utterly and completely free from your job! Yes the next three weeks will be stressful and yes money will be tight for a little while but you will be SO HAPPY once you're out of here. I know it was hard for you to hold back the tears in the meeting with all of your bosses today, but you did good kid! Look at how much you've been smiling the rest of the day today!

Take the rest of November one day at a time and prepare for your great adventure with Stevie! You are FREE!

Also, I'm proud of you for voting for the first time today. I know it is bittersweet for you to vote in a state you will soon be leaving, but this will be good for the Country.

Remember there will be hard days to come where you will want to text J... Don't. This is your time now and you're not ready to speak to him anyway. Take care of that pup and be good to yourself. Your life dream just got real! Remember the last time you did something similar everything worked out so well in your favor and it will work out in your favor again. When you start to freak out about the future recite these three words: 'I AM FREE!'

Love,

Your crazy gut feelings that make you do scary shit.

NOVEMBER 8, 2018

Asking For a Friend - Devin Dawson

Dear Big 95 5 Listeners,

Tonight was my last night hosting a concert with you guys and you had no clue. But it was PERFECT. Never in a million years did I think I could stand onstage in Chicago of all places and hear people yell 'Alabama' to me like you did tonight. You made me feel so special when you'd walk up and ask for a photo and tell me a story about what was going on in your life when you'd listen to certain segments I did on the radio.

You by far have made me feel more welcome in this city than anywhere I've ever lived and I will always miss that. I feel like we've been through so much together on the radio here. From working mornings and afternoons at the same time which was one of the most excruciating work schedules of my life to crying over my mom's addiction on air and you calling me to share your stories of someone in your life battling addiction. It's been special to have my grandmother who raised me on the air and you loving Meemaw as much as I do. You followed along my 'Year of Bama' where I spent an entire year focusing on bettering myself and you even rooted for me when I had a major surgery that scared me to death.

I feel like we have grown so much together and I will forever be grateful for that. I don't know if my travels in life will ever bring me back to Chicago but I'd like to think they will one day. It's weird to say that you actually do feel like my family and somehow Chicago has come to feel more like home than I ever expected. I had an amazing time with you tonight and I just wanted to say Thank you for allowing me to be a part of your life this past four years. It has been an honor.

Love you,

Alabama

NOVEMBER 11, 2018

Tequila Sunrise - Eagles

Dear Tequila,

I hate you. The hangover I'm feeling today makes me NEVER want to drink again. Why do I even go out when I already know by the end of the night I'll be annoyed with the Chicago weekend crowd that invades my city. It's basically a ton of creepy drunk guys trying to impress the slutty dressed drunk girls by buying bottle service and acting like they can sit at their table if they are lucky enough to catch his eye. None of those guys ever let me sit at their table when I was one of those slutty dressed drunk girls! I don't think they really understood my Alabama sense of humor. Or the fact that I was too blunt and would call them out on their ridiculousness.

Oh well, it doesn't matter anymore since I'll be gone soon and in the woods. No need to worry about dressing up to go out or if I'll fall in the snow if I wear four-inch heels or even worrying if I fit into those tiny club dresses anymore. I won't even have to shave my legs if I don't want to! I wish I was there already!

At least I had fun with Danielle last night! That's where I started to make the bad decision to drink you last night! At Nicks Beer Garden in Wicker Park where some worker there kept buying us shots of you! He particularly thought it was funny when we kept begging him to show us where the secret doorway was to some hidden alley so that we could smoke our cigarettes and drink our beer. He told us to 'hide our beers in our coats' and follow him. I thought it was hysterical when he just led us out the front door and around the corner to drink our beers and have our cigarettes… I could have walked us out the damn front door too guy! What a trick!

43

I'm really going to miss my girls nights out with Danielle... I wish I would have had more girls nights out while I lived here. That was one of the things I actually learned how to enjoy in my 30's after moving to Chicago.

Before Chicago, I'd always had more guy friends than girls which usually ended up being a disaster because one or both of us ultimately wanted to more than just friends. I had no idea what I was missing with girls nights and bonding about how dumb guys can be.

Anyway, tequila you suck! I'm pretty sure I drunk texted him last night (which I won't even open to see what I said), I slept all day today and it hurts to get up and take Stevie out for a walk. At least I'm too hungover to smoke a cigarette so maybe today will be the day I quit. Thanks for that!

Gonna go puke now,

Amber

NOVEMBER 16, 2018

· ·

The Weight - Aretha Franklin

Dear Clare Dunn,

I am so happy we spoke tonight! I didn't realize how much of a soul sister you really are until the third time we met! Thank you for listening to my stories about my wild ass great grand-mother and how she used to sell speed to truckers in the '70s! She's one of my favorite people in the world and one of the reasons I'm thinking about moving back home after this trip. She's not getting any younger and I want to spend more time with her before she's gone.

And thank you for being so supportive of the journey I'm going to take! It's so crazy to me that you are so excited for me when I'm more excited about your journey as an artist. You are such a talented woman and I cannot wait for you to blow up even bigger than you already are. I wish I had the balls to do what you do every night onstage. If I'm telling you the truth tonight being an artist like you has actually always been my childhood dream.

Ha! I appreciate you for offering to get me a gun on this trip too! I'm still laughing at you asking me what my Venmo name was and instead I decided to share my location with you indefinitely so you can check in on me during the trip. I promise I will be safe! I have a machete and bear spray!

I hope our paths will cross again soon. You truly do feel like a soul sister and I appreciate you.

Alabama

NOVEMBER 21, 2018

Turns Out That Way - The Rewinds

Dear Lauren,

It's odd that I'm writing to you because 10 years ago the thought of even speaking to you wasn't an option. But here we are 10 years later, both burned by the same guy and bonding over it!

It's weird to think that I was once engaged to a guy so long ago and how devastated I was when he married you so soon after we broke up. I was so heartbroken over him that I packed my life up in Alabama and moved all the way across the country to get over it. That ended up being the best thing I ever did for myself. If I didn't get out of this town I'd have never gotten a job in radio and gotten to do all of the amazing things I have done with my life the past decade.

You and I used to have this weird disdain for each other whenever I'd come to town. I hated you because you had him and I'm sure you hated me because when you first started dating I was still calling him wanting to win him back. I'm glad you recognized me tonight though and we had a high five over finally getting away from him and his toxic behaviors!

It's sad really... strong women fall in love with the wrong guys all the time and instead of seeing what the guy is doing wrong we tend to blame it on the other women they date. It isn't until the guy really burns us down that we see it was them all along. I'm glad you are happy and I think in another life you and I would have actually been great friends. You said I look happy tonight and I haven't felt happy in a long time but maybe I am starting to be happy again... finally!

Thanks for saying hello tonight!

Sincerely,

Your ex-husband's ex-fiancé

NOVEMBER 27, 2018

Bathroom Sink - Miranda Lambert

Dear Dexter and Dixie,

I miss you two!!! I'm sorry that you're in a new place and Angie is a stranger to you but she loves cats and she will love you just like you are her very own babies! I'll be gone for a few weeks to go on a trip but I'm sure you will appreciate the break from Stevie chasing you around the house for a while. I told Angie not to give you any more baths because I know you hate them!

I freaked out when she sent me the video of you both getting a bath and told her we leave that to the professionals. I think she forgot that you are deaf Dexter when she said in the video of her bathing you to 'Let the world hear you cry.' Haha, Angie really is one of a kind!

I promise I will come back and get you both when I get a new home for us! I just need to go out into the world right now and do this for myself and figure out where really feels like home… I can't answer that right now but hopefully, I'll know sooner than later. I miss you more than you know and I'll see you soon!

Love,

Mom

NOVEMBER 28, 2018

The Night We Met - Lord Huron

Dear J,

I don't really know why I'm writing you right now. Sometimes you feel like a distant memory and other times it feels like you were just here yesterday. I just ate the cream cheese you bought the last time you were here and planned on making some sort of weird pie. I keep seeing pictures of you with her on Facebook and you look happy but that makes me so sad because I wonder why I couldn't make you that happy. Then I think about you bringing her to Thanksgiving with your family and that's a whole other can of worms because I thought you and I would be spending the holidays together this year. I love your family so much.

I'm so ready to just be over this breakup but I'm afraid to move on because I don't want to forget what it felt like to love you. Loving you just felt right, like everything was falling into place in my life and I had finally found the best friend I had been waiting on to spend the rest of my life with. The more time that passes between us makes me think that maybe the love I thought we had really was just all in my head and you never felt the same way about me. Then the thought of that being true breaks my heart all over again. It's just so hard to make sense of what happened. It felt like one day you were telling me you were in love with me and wanted to move in together and have this happy life then the next day you were leaving me for someone else. I want to hate you for what happened but when I really think about it I just can't bring myself to.

I wish you could see Stevie now. She's doubled her weight at 60 pounds and has the funniest personality. You'd love her even more than you did when I first got her if that's possible. I'm not going to lie there was a time right after we broke up that I considered taking her back to the shelter because I was so upset over you it became difficult for me to even get up and take her out for a walk some days. But I kept getting up and taking her out and she kept cuddling me on the hard nights that I spent crying over you.

I thought she would be a constant reminder of you and the future I thought we would have together but really she became my best friend throughout this breakup and now I no longer look at her as what would have been our dog... She is my new best friend. Thank you for that.

Amber

NOVEMBER 30, 2018

Long Nights - Eddie Vedder

Dear Friends and Family,

I have felt lost for a while now. I think I may have been this way ever since I was a little girl and my parents chose drugs and abusive relationships over me. I could never understand why they couldn't love me enough for us to be a happy family together. My whole life I've been searching for something to fill that hole inside of me and have yet to be successful.

I've been looking for love and happiness in all the wrong places. It's almost masochistic that I chose a career that consists of trying to make thousands of people love me on a daily basis. The truth is, in my search for love I lost myself and then slowly over time began to resent who I had become. I stopped following my heart and separated myself from my true dreams. Sometimes I don't even recognize myself anymore.

After a ton of preparation and many conversations with people who think I've gone completely off the deep end, I've decided to take a break from it all. This is one of the toughest decisions I've ever made. I'm leaving one of the greatest jobs of my career, putting all of my stuff in storage and leaving everything as I know it behind.

I've packed my car with only the necessities: my dog and a tent. We're going to travel the country together and do some soul searching. Don't worry if you don't hear from me for a while, it just means I'm out in the wild with my dog enjoying life in a way I never have before. Don't worry we have survival gear and bear spray so I'll be okay!

Thank you for being so supportive of my career and life choices. I don't know where this journey will lead me or what my life will become afterward but when the time is right I will let you know.

Until we meet again,

Amber

DECEMBER 3, 2018

This Conversation - Ciaran Lavery

Dear Chicago,

Leaving you was hands down one of the toughest decisions of my life. When I first moved here I remember the cab drivers telling me, "Welcome to the best city in the world!" In that moment I had no idea how right they were. From smiling my biggest grin along to Chance the Rapper at Lollapalooza, beaming after meeting Ben Gibbard from Death Cab For Cutie at the Chicago Theatre, to getting stuck on the Ferris wheel while No Doubt was playing at Riot Fest and then falling in love with the people here after walking onstage and hearing them yell my name while I was making announcements at Windy City Smokeout.

The moments I spent in this city always left me in awe. From the architecture tour on the river in the summer to watching the river turn neon green on Saint Patricks Day. Being on the water in Chicago is one of the most magical places to be.

I found a huge part of myself in this city. I never imagined that a girl from Pinson Alabama would move into a high rise in downtown Chicago and learn how to navigate the hustle of a large city and fall in love with the movement all around me. I don't know if my life will ever bring me back here to live but I do know it will always be a home I can come back to and visit and I am forever grateful for that.

I will always love you Chicago.

Alabama

DECEMBER 4, 2018

Althea - Grateful Dead

Dear Holly and Roberto,

Thank you for letting Stevie and me crash on your couch! I can tell Stevie had a lot of fun running around in your yard. I know it can be a pain having a dog AND a person take over your personal space, especially when Stevie would follow you around begging for food so I truly appreciate you both for being so kind and letting us into your home. I'm amazed at how good she was when I set up the hammock in your yard and stayed next to me for over an hour with no leash. Hopefully, she will do the same once we are really out in the wild!

Stevie really loves you Holly, but please don't feed her any more

Amber Cole

sandwich meat… the aftermath was NO FUN to deal with!

Roberto, you can play my guitars whenever you want! When I get back from my trip I will teach you more songs to play.

Holly you have always been someone I've looked up to and I'm so happy that I have you as a wild hippy woman in my life to show me how it is supposed to be lived! I hope my adventures as an adult make you a proud aunt. I'm so happy that you found Roberto, you two seem happy. You are some of the kindest people I know and I love you both for that.

Love you.

Amber

DECEMBER 6, 2018

For What it's Worth - Buffalo Springfield

Dear Peepaw,

Thank you for telling me stories about when you were in Vietnam and living in the jungle a long time ago. When I'm out in the woods and get scared I'll remember that you did it during a war and it will give me comfort in knowing that I can do this too. It made me giggle how excited you got over my portable solar-powered shower and my first aid kit with a venom sucker in case I get bit by a snake. I might have over prepared but I'd rather be ready for anything than not prepared at all.

It meant the world to me that you have been one of the few people that hasn't said I'm crazy for what I'm about to do. You gave me the best advice tonight when I was asking you a million questions about surviving in the woods and you finally stopped me and said, "You can worry about all that stuff all you want but you just have to go do it, enjoy life while you're out there and have fun." Honestly, I didn't expect that advice to come from you. I'd been waiting for you to scold me all week but then you were excited about my trip and I was taken by surprise. I appreciate that more than you know.

Thank you for helping to raise me into the woman I have become and setting an example for the type of man I hope to marry one day. Thank you for supporting my wild heart and encouraging me to be free.

I love you Peepaw,

Amber

DECEMBER 7, 2018

I'm With You - Vance Joy

Dear J,

Part of me hates being home right now because all I want to do is text you to come see Stevie and me. But I know you won't and I can't handle another letdown. I passed you driving through Pinson today and for some reason, I thought you would have seen me and said something... but not a word.

I asked the universe for a sign if we would end up together again and at first passing you the next day seemed like a good sign. But the more I think about it, we were headed in opposite directions and I think THAT was the sign. We are both going in two different directions with our lives. I'm still looking for somewhere bigger that feels like home and I thought that was going to be with you traveling all over the world but the reality is you want to stay here because it's your home. I can't take you away from that. Dragging you away from somewhere you love just to be with me is selfish. That is not love.

I'm glad that I'm stuck in Alabama for a few weeks waiting on my movers because being here is making me remember why I left in the first place. This isn't my home anymore. What you don't know about the day you broke up with me is that morning I asked my job to let me move back to Alabama so that I could be with you. I could feel your growing uneasiness to move to Chicago and I loved you so much that I was willing to leave that all behind to come back home and have a life with you here. Now that I'm here I realize that I wouldn't have been happy if that actually happened. After the honeymoon phase wore off I probably would have resented you for coming back here with nothing to do.

I'll admit being so close to you right now and knowing that you don't care is crushing my heart a little more but it's also helping me to move on. If you really loved me and it was just the distance that broke us then you'd want to see me now that I'm here. I'm not sad anymore and I'm starting to feel indifferent. The more I try to make sense of everything the more I realize I actually do deserve better. I knew when we started dating that you were struggling to be the best version of yourself and I was dumb to think that somehow I could help you with that. Love isn't a game of fixing someone else. We have to fix ourselves before we can actually be happy with someone else. Hell, I think I still have some work on myself to do before I'm ready to be in a relationship and make it work too. I think that's the biggest lesson I took away from this relationship. I hope you are well.

Amber

DECEMBER 8, 2018

Love Hurts - Incubus

Dear Stevie,

I'm so grateful for you! I feel like an asshole for not loving you at first sight. When you first came out of your cage at the shelter you were this wild hyper puppy and I thought, "She's going to be one of the bad ones." Then we got home and I realized I was so wrong. I still thought I would give you back when my two weeks of fostering you were up, but then J fell in love with you too and I just knew you were meant to be our dog.

I'm sorry when he broke up with me that I stayed on my couch for days and stopped taking you on long trips to the park. You stayed right by me that entire week and together we got through it. Then when I started taking you to the park again you were just this happy puppy that went up to every stranger for a pet and you got me talking to people again. Thank you for that.

I'm sorry that right now I've uprooted you from your routine with this adventure we are about to go on. At first, I thought we'd be outside all the time and you'd love all the space. It wasn't until we started couch surfing in Alabama this past week that I realized how I've not only made myself homeless but now you are homeless too and that isn't fair.

I wanted to get so mad at you the other day for eating my Birkenstock, but I know you did it because you are confused about your new surroundings and I can't get mad at you for that. The cool thing that came out of it is Birkenstock lets you buy one shoe and they donate the other to an amputee organization. So we actually did a little bit of good together!

I realized tonight that the reason I dated J was to bring me to you. At first, I thought he was in my life to teach me some sort of lesson about love but the truth is without him I probably wouldn't have kept you and now I am SO grateful that I did. You have become my child, my protector, my shadow and my best friend.

I'm sorry I didn't bond with you right away but now I cannot imagine life without you. I know I 'rescued' you but you have rescued me in so many other ways. I wouldn't be doing this trip if I didn't have you with me, I'd be too afraid. Thank you for being the best companion a girl could ever ask for.

I love you,

Mom

DECEMBER 12, 2018

Radio - Sylvan Esso

Dear Angie (and Justin),

Thank you for letting Stevie and me come over for a few days on top of watching my cats. I felt bad that all four of us have taken over your house this week. I can't believe that sweet little deaf cat Dexter has started picking on your cats that are three times his size! My favorite thing this week was our dance party in the living room where Stevie jumped in. She didn't know what the hell we were doing but she definitely danced with us!

I'm sorry Stevie pooped in your basement, I don't know when the little shit snuck down there to do that. I did catch her down there once eating the cat litter like there was no tomorrow, but definitely not pooping.

Angie, picking pecans at your dad's house was so good for my soul today. I forgot how intertwined our childhoods were that your family feels like my family and my family is your family too. We really are sisters. Tell your dad, 'Thank you!' for the motorcycle ride. You are so lucky to have such an amazing father that loves you as much as he does. I've always envied that about you. I'm so happy that you two have each other and I appreciate the fact that you and your family has been a part of my life since I was five years old. You are so much more than just a friend and I cannot thank you enough for being so supportive of this next journey my life is taking.

I love you,

Amber

DECEMBER 13, 2018

Hard Sun - Eddie Vedder

Dear Movers,

Please hurry up with my stuff! The constant delay is putting such a huge damper on my trip and I'm tired of couch surfing in my home town. My friends and family are annoyed with Stevie and me, and I'm sick of being reminded of him. Everywhere I look I'm reminded of him and the fact that I'm finally close to him and he wants nothing to do with me. You'd think being home would feel great but I have nowhere to go and no one wants me around. I'm ready to be in the woods with my dog and away from everything.

Sincerely,

Irritated customer

DECEMBER 17, 2018

Heavy - Bird Talker

Dear Alabama,

I'm glad my trip got delayed and I spent two weeks home but man was it HARD. I realized that I left a lot of heartache in Birmingham when I moved away 12 years ago. From the hearts that I broke to the people here that broke my heart. Even radio almost broke me here because no one would hire me when I knew if someone would just give me a chance I'd be amazing on air. I got a chance doing what I love everywhere else BUT here. Even now that I'm here and trying to find a job no one will hire me. It's strange how I still feel like such an outsider in my home-town. The place that is supposed to bring me comfort brings me too much pain.

Some have said that I'm running away from my problems and no matter where I go my problems will follow me. Those people have never gone into the woods to be with themselves and their problems alone to sort through them and work them out. I've been sad for a long time and I intend to stay out there until I camp the sad out of me.

Thank you for making me who I am Alabama, but now I must go find who I am supposed to be.

Love,

Amber

Day #1 - Cypress Creek - DeSoto National Forest, Mississippi

DECEMBER 18, 2018

Let You Down - NF

Dear Friends and Family,

I'm just two days into this trip and it's already scaring the shit out of me. Last night was terrifying and I almost turned around and came right back home. I stayed in the middle of nowhere DeSoto National Forest which seemed great during the day because Stevie and I were the only living creatures for hours and that was what I wanted right? Well, night came. We heard coyotes and I thought that would scare us, but it wasn't their shrill cries or the squeaking of the moles that scared us at all. I didn't even flinch when I heard footsteps of whatever animals were snooping around right outside my tent.

It was the people who drove out to the abandoned campground in the middle of the night that scared the hell out of me. No ranger marking on the truck and it flew around a fast circle like it already knew the lay of the land. They had definitely been there before. I thought when they flew back out of the entrance of the campground they had realized people were camping and they would leave. Then they turned off their headlights and parked.

What the hell were they doing? I sat in my car with Stevie, my bear spray, and a gun next to me just staring into the darkness and waiting. Minutes felt like hours and then the gunshots happened.

Fuck that! I started the car and flew out of there as fast as I could! I don't know if the gunshots were from that truck or across the river but it was not worth waiting and finding out. I left the tent and all of my belongings at that campsite and drove twenty miles to the nearest hotel.

I did call the rangers station this morning to see if there was any way it could have been a ranger checking on the campground last night. The lady politely told me it was not a ranger, then went on to scold me for ten more minutes about camping alone with no cell phone service. Pretty sure I'm going to exclude that story from the conversation when I check in with Meemaw later.

All day long I keep asking myself what the hell am I doing and all I can think about is him and did I do everything I could have to keep him from leaving me. If so would I even be out in the middle of the woods right now almost getting myself killed?

Obviously, the only sane thing to do was text him asking if he was 100% sure he made the right choice…. Who knew that the phrase, "I'm sorry but I am," could feel so paralyzing on the way to my next campsite. I know I need to hear that so I can really just move on from him but this stings. How could I have been so sure about someone who wasn't really sure about me? And now I feel like a crazy person for being so upset that I left my job and a city that I love to basically go be homeless and 'find myself' in the woods and get over a dumb boy. Why do I take breakups so personally when I just need to accept what is and move on in a normal way. I could have eaten some cookie dough and drank a bottle of wine and cried over a Nicholas Sparks movie instead of completely flipping my life upside down. This seems so absurd now that I'm writing out the truth of what I'm doing.

I hate my parents for screwing me up as much as they did. The root of all my issues goes back to being abandoned as a child and never feeling good enough for them. Will I ever really learn how to love in a healthy way?

Oh, and did I mention I pulled a fucking tick off my arm tonight! That alone makes me want to strip down, check myself all over for these Lyme disease-carrying bastards then drive right back to Alabama and sleep in a warm bed away from bugs.

At least I'm staying at a KOA in Lafayette tonight. It's well lit, surrounded by people and there are showers, a laundry mat, camp store and most of all it is SAFE. It's right by the freeway but at least the sunset was still pretty even if there were 18 wheelers driving in front of it. Plus there are trees to hang my hammock and a grill to cook actual food on so I'm happy.

I might stay here two nights to give Stevie a break from being in the car and myself a break from setting up the tent again. I didn't realize how much work this actually is. By the time I get camp set up night comes and I'm too exhausted to relax. I don't think I really knew what to expect when I planned this. Hopefully, it will get better the further west I go, but I think I'll stick to KOA's for a while.

Thank you for checking in on me and sorry for not responding to every text asking how we are doing, just know I'm trying to figure this hole in my heart out and I will come home once I am whole again.

I love you.

Amber

Night #2 - KOA - Lafayette, Louisiana- Campsite #49

DECEMBER 19, 2018

· ·

Fake You - Yoke Lore

Dear J,

I don't even know where to begin. You texting me last night that the time we spent together wasn't taken lightly and that you do love me seems like such bull shit. If that were true how could you have lied to me the way you did for so long?

I woke up this morning and had an image in my head that you are actually happier with her than you ever were with me and it broke my heart all over again. I don't want to keep reliving this breakup but I can't get it out of my head. This morning will be the last time that I cry over you. Not because I hate you but because I need to get over you. I can't keep going over everything in my mind anymore and asking myself how this happened. Did you do the same thing to her with me when we first started dating? There were so many red flags that I ignored because I thought you were the one. In my mind, it was like I had known my soulmate all along and we finally came together after all these years when the timing was right. I'm letting go of that idea now because it was just what I wanted to see in that moment.

I keep telling myself that I've been lost the past few months after our breakup, but I realized today that it's you who is lost. I never felt like I was good enough for you. Now that I'm looking back at it I was more than enough I just wasn't her. I'm not blaming that on anyone, I just wish now that I would have paid attention to all the signs.

I should have spoken up and said something. It makes me sad that you're missing all of this. I used to imagine that you and I would travel the world together like I am now and I know deep in your heart you were meant to roam the world and be so much more than you are letting yourself be now. I hope you don't settle for less because you're too afraid to make the jump.

If you do I will be so mad at you because I know for a fact the life we would have had together would have been extraordinary and if you gave that up to be ordinary I will never forgive you. Well, I will... but I'll still be disappointed knowing what could have been.

Until next time,

Amber

DECEMBER 19, 2018

Proud Mary - Creedence Clearwater Revival

Dear Aunt Mary,

Thank you for teaching me how to sew when I was a kid! I thought about the hours you spent teaching me how to cross stitch and sew pillows when I was 10 years old today. I used those skills to stitch a hole in my tent that I somehow managed to rip on my third day of camping. Probably not how you imagined me using a needle and thread when you bought my first sewing machine, but it came in handy! I'll have another day of keeping bugs out of my home thanks to you! You'd be proud I used orange thread to match my tent.

You were such an amazing adult in my life growing up and it

makes me sad that I haven't seen you in over ten years. I'll never forget you taking me to a breast cancer walk while you worked the booth as a survivor. I've heard that all the treatment you've gone through has been hard on your body the past few years and I'm so sorry that you had to endure that. Now that I'm grown I can see how big it was that you would babysit me and teach me everything that you did while you were going through such a hard time in your life. I didn't understand that as a child.

You are heavy on my mind tonight and I promise I will make a point to come visit you and show you my stitchwork after this trip!

I appreciate you,

Amber

Night #3 - KOA campground - Lafayette, Louisiana - Campsite #49

DECEMBER 19, 2018

Beware the Dog - The Grizwolds

Dear Stevie,

You are not the easiest dog in the world to go camping with! I think I've said, "No!" and "What are you doing!?" more times than I can count. The firewood is not a chew toy! The picnic table is not for climbing! Pine cones are not a ball to play fetch with!

But I wouldn't have it any other way.

Love,

Mom

DECEMBER 20, 2018

One Night in the Sun - LP

Dear Friends and Family,

It's great out here. I finally feel free.

Love,

Amber

Night #4 - New Braunfels Texas - Cory's house

DECEMBER 21, 2018

Dreamcatcher - LP

Dear Cory,

Thank you so much for opening up your home to Stevie and me! I hope Stevie was good practice for you when you finally decide to get a dog! She definitely had fun playing fetch in your backyard and sneaking onto your couch when we weren't looking.

Thank you for showing me around Gruene! I'm excited about the pumpkin peanut butter I bought for this trip but now I wish I'd had also grabbed the jalapeño peanut butter we tried at the General Store. Next time I come back we have to go back to the speakeasy that you showed me... Definitely, my favorite place we visited so far.

I know I kept avoiding your advances towards me while I stayed and I didn't know how to tell you I'm just not over my breakup yet. Any other time or if we lived in the same place I might have tried to date you. You are such a great guy and I think it's amazing how handy you are. I was amazed the last time we hung out and you showed me the tiny house you were starting to build. I'd have made you finish it so we could travel the world together in it! In another life, we could have been happy. But this is this life and my heart belongs to someone else.

Thank you for being you and I hope that you find a girl that will make you happy one day. If not a girl then at least a dog like Stevie! It will be so worth it.

Until I see you again,

Amber

Night #5 - New Braunfels, Texas

DECEMBER 22, 2018

Kin - Penny and Sparrow

Dear Aunt Kathy,

Thank you so much for letting Stevie and I come to visit for a few days! I know I haven't seen you since I was a little kid, but getting to spend time with you and my cousins felt like home to me. I saw so much of myself in you guys and it completely blew me away. How could this family that I haven't known for over thirty years be so free-spirited and wild at heart just like me?

You are such an amazing woman and a kindred soul. I love your wild and playful heart. Never lose that. I'm in awe of how kind and giving you are. From how patient you are with your animals (and my Stevie who chewed up a box of oatmeal, sorry about that!), to seeing how kind and caring your kids have grown up to be. You are one of the most genuine souls I've met, and the world needs more people like you in it. I cannot thank you enough for showing me the love and compassion that you did when I needed it the most.

It didn't feel like Christmas to me this year until I came to your home, and we drove around looking at Christmas lights and baked Cowboy cookies. Thank you for bringing the Christmas spirit back into my heart this year... It is one of my favorite times of the year and it was starting to bother me that I couldn't get into the mood to celebrate.

It's been bothering me for years that I couldn't relate to anyone on my father's side of the family. I've been estranged from him for years but even when I did speak to him I felt like he was such a foreign thing to me. I never understood him and I felt like I just didn't belong in that part of the family, but finally getting to spend time with you brought me so much joy knowing that you understand me and love me with no judgment. This visit was better for my soul than I could have ever realized.

I love you and I cannot wait to see you again soon!

Amber Brooke

Night #6 - Big Spring, Texas

DECEMBER 23, 2018

Giants - Bear Hands

Dear Destinie,

I think you have just become one of my favorite cousins in the world! I'm amazed at your kindness towards animals and I think it is so cool that you work for animal control. The way you find a way to save every animal you come in contact with is one of the things I love about you the most. Still, my favorite story about you is how you fed a bear s'mores when your mom took you camping as a little kid. I can just imagine the terror on her face when she saw you walk over to a log and lay the snack on it and a huge bear appear from nowhere and stand up and eat it while you thought it was a normal thing! I'm really surprised Aunt Kathy took you camping again after that! Ha!

It blows my mind how similar we are even though we never grew up near each other. I'm so glad that we finally got to meet as adults and I feel like we've just become friends instead of distant cousins. Once I find out where my next home will be, please come visit me anytime!

Riding Hank today was just what I needed. He's such an amazing horse (even if he did bite me!) Just being at the stables and being able to see all of the animals were good for my soul and I think you knew that it would be. I'll definitely remember catching my first baby goat and making friends with a cow today! For the first time in a while, I forgot that I was sad and got to enjoy being around these animals and feel a little bit of joy. Thank you so much for that.

I love you!

Amber

Night #7 - Big Spring Texas

DECEMBER 23, 2018

For All the Cows - Foo Fighters

Dear Chip,

I promise to never eat you! Meemaw always teases me for being a vegetarian but playing with you today just reaffirmed why I chose to stop eating meat a few years ago. You act like a big puppy! How could I ever think it is okay to raise something with such a big personality only to take its life and eat it later? I never thought about that before, but now that I'm older I'm realizing more and more how precious every single life on this planet is. What right do I have to decide which of God's creations have a more meaningful life than others? I just can't do it.

Especially you and your big personality! You kind of reminded me of a big toddler trying to play with Destinie and I. You reminded me of being a toddler myself, and going with Nanny to her brother's house to feed his baby cow with a bottle almost as big as me!

Now that I'm thinking about it, I should thank Nanny for that experience. She always supported my love for animals whether we were going to visit her brother's cows or if I caught a stray cat and she let me keep it as a pet at her house.

Anyway Chip, I'm glad we met! Next time I'll bring more treats for you so you don't have to follow me all over the field begging for more! But please stop butting me with your horns, they hurt! You don't realize how big you are!

Love,

Your new friend

DECEMBER 23, 2018

Different - Hippie Sabotage

Dear Marcus,

Hey! You didn't think your mom and sister would be the only ones with letters, do you? I hope one day you realize how amazing you truly are. I know being different can feel difficult most of the time, but trust me when I say that you are not alone. Many people in the world struggle to fit in and sometimes people will try so hard to fit in that they sacrifice who they are just to belong to the wrong group of people. I've tried so hard to fit in and make people like me that there were times I didn't even recognize myself anymore. I got so far away from who I was that I started to resent the person I had become.

My point is, your differences are a special gift. You are brilliant in your own special ways and the fact that you are so brutally honest is refreshing. Plus your sense of humor is funnier than most people I know. I think we are all supposed to be different so that we can all learn from each other. Some of my best friends in life are my polar opposite and we end up fitting together like two puzzle pieces. We help each other grow. I think that is the point of life sometimes. And I think that you have so much to offer the world that more people need in their life. You even helped me grow this weekend when I visited!

It's easy to get caught up on the things about ourselves that we perceive to be flaws and we forget to use our strengths to our advantage. I hope you look at the things that are good in yourself more because you are way more awesome than a lot of people I know. You will be successful in life, I can tell! The world needs more people like you in it. You make it a much better place just by existing.

Amber Cole

Love,

Amber

Jolene - Lay Low

Dear Girl,

I've been waiting to write this letter because frankly, I didn't want to believe that you were actually with him, but after seeing photos of you spending Christmas Eve with his family I can't ignore reality anymore. That was the worst because a few months ago it was supposed to be me coming back home to Alabama for the holidays happy with him and our families. But now I'm in the middle of nowhere New Mexico with my dog on Christmas Eve in an empty hotel and feeling lost.

I don't know how much you know about him and I but I imagine it's very little since he didn't say a word about you until it was all said and done. It's weird that he never mentioned you and I still had a dream that he was hiding you from me the night before he broke up with me. My heart knew what he was doing before my mind even realized it.

You and I were friends once in high school and honestly before we even became friends I admired you from afar while we were growing up together in grade school. You were a lot like me in so many ways but I felt like I wasn't brave enough or pretty enough to just be myself like you always seemed to be. I'm trying so hard to be the bigger person in all of this and not have ill feelings towards you over a boy, so I have to believe that he didn't tell you the full story of he and I when he left me for you. That's okay too, you don't need to know the full story, but I will say this… I loved him more than I thought I could love a person. It surprised and scared me how fast he popped back into my life and how hurt I was over what he did.

I do believe that everything happens for a reason and if he and I were meant to be together then we would have been and if you are meant to be with him then you will work out and be fine. But please don't hurt him. When I found out about you, I instantly thought about the baby the two mothers were fighting over and King Solomon said to cut the baby in half and they would both have a baby. One of the mothers said no. She would rather her baby be whole and alive even if it was with another mother. I will not cut J in half. If being with you is what makes him whole I will find a way to accept it and eventually be happy for the both of you.

I just hope you love him as deeply as I did and would have. Inspire him to be the man he already is but doesn't see in himself yet. Make him laugh when he is sad. Tell him he is handsome every day. Go explore the world with him. Give him control of the radio when you're in the car. Get a dog for him to love on. He misses his old dog and I think it will be good for his soul. Kiss him when he's frustrated. Be all the things I wanted to be for him and be even better at all the things I couldn't be for him. Don't let this heartache I'm going through be for nothing. Keep him whole.

Amber

Night #8 - Christmas Eve - Clayton, New Mexico - Best Western - room #123

DECEMBER 25, 2018

No One's Gonna Love You - Band of Horses

Dear Baby,

A year ago today I became pregnant with you and had no idea. Some would have called it a Christmas miracle but for me, it was sort of my own personal hell. You see I had a tumor on my uterus that was the size of a cantaloupe and the universe just wasn't lined up for me to have you yet. It's ironic because when I first found out about my tumor I was terrified that I would never be able to have kids after having it removed, then I got pregnant with you against all odds. I couldn't have you because I needed to have that tumor removed and that killed me inside. I wanted to be a mother so badly to you.

I had been so afraid for years that I would be a terrible mother because I never really had a good example in my own mother. I was so afraid that if I ever had kids I wouldn't know what to do and my motherly instincts wouldn't kick in. But now I'm starting to think I might actually be a decent one someday.

You would be three months old today and Stevie would be your big (puppy) sister. I'd like to think that you two would have grown up together and looked out for each other. This would have been your first Christmas and I'd have spoiled you so much. I bet Meemaw and Peepaw would have to. This has been a hard day for me to celebrate because I keep thinking about you and the significance of today.

Love,

Mom

Night #9 - Boulder, Colorado

DECEMBER 28, 2018

On the Road Again - Willie Nelson

Dear Stevie,

I promise when I get my next job I'll get an SUV so you'll have more space on our future road trips. I know today's drive was long and hard and you hated being cramped inside my tiny Volkswagen Beetle. I felt so guilty when you'd keep popping your head in between the two front seats and dropping your ball in my lap wanting to play. Thank you for being such a good road warrior this trip.

Love,

Mom

Day #12 - The drive from Boulder, Colorado to Moab, Utah

DECEMBER 28, 2018

Wild Horses (Acoustic) - Bishop Briggs

Dear Trevor,

Your house was one I didn't want to leave on this road trip but I know that I have to keep moving on. It is so crazy to me now that I'm looking back at how heartbroken I was when you moved away from Chicago two years ago. I had such strong feelings for you back then and over the past two years I had gotten over you, but it blew my mind that I was still nervous around you this visit. There were a few times that I thought about the last guy that broke my heart and wondered if I would ever get to the point that I'm over it and we can be friends again like I am with you now. I have to admit that I am really grateful for your friendship now and there was a time in my life that I thought we could never be friends.

There are still some times that I wonder if you and I could still end up together. Our lives keep crossing paths and I keep wondering what is this bond that keeps pushing us back together. I felt like we never had a major relationship so what is it that makes me still feel so attached to you at times? Is there something bigger in our story that I'm just not seeing yet? It's easy to let my mind wander about all of these things after seeing you and spending all day on the road today. It was such a nice break to spend Christmas with you this year and I appreciate you letting Stevie and I into your home. I think we are bonded in the fact that we both can feel so alone and estranged from our families at times. In a way, you have started to feel like my family now. Isn't it funny how people can bond over similar misfortunes?

Oh and my ass still hurts from you teaching me how to snowboard the other day! I can't believe we made it out of those mountains in the snowstorm leaving the ski lodge. That was hands down the scariest drive of my life. I'll never live on a mountain for that one reason! I wish you were on this trip with me for a few days. The drive through The Rockies into Utah was the most beautiful part of this road trip so far! It felt like driving through a scene in the movies and I know you would have loved it. Moab is even more beautiful than I'd imagined it. I would live here if I could. The people are all explorers and love adventure like you and I do. The town has an adventurous feel to it, a ton of fun shops to visit, and it's surrounded by the most amazing landscape. You'd love it here.

Maybe one day we will live in the same place again and we can spend more time together. I appreciate your gypsy soul and thank you again for letting Stevie and I make your home our home for a few days.

Until next time,

Amber

Night # 12 - Moab, Utah - Motel 6 - Room #118

DECEMBER 28, 2018

Good as Hell - Lizzo

Dear Mary,

I thought about you a lot the past few days. Mainly because I need a facial and a massage more than I've ever needed before! You'd yell at me if you saw how bad I need a spa day and pedicure. I will NEVER take pedicures for granted ever again!

It's funny, you see someone for random hygiene maintenance for two years and slowly over time that person becomes your friend without you even realizing it. I specifically remember one of the first massages I got from you and opening up about my mother's drug addiction and you sharing similar life stories

Amber Cole

and I thought, 'This girl just gets me.'

In a way, you have been there through all of my big life events for the past two years. My dating horror stories, my surgery, weight loss, career moves and more. You have truly become a friend to me and I'm realizing today how much I miss you for more than just coming to you for a spa day. I'm going to miss the bond we had with each other.

I love your fiery spirit! Don't ever change that about yourself. You are a face to be reckoned with and screw anyone who tries to put that fire out!

Thank you for being you!

Amber

PS. I don't think I'll ever find anyone else that I trust to wax my lady bits again, so can you just travel to me once a month?!?! Ha! (But seriously... can you?)

DECEMBER 29, 2018

The Scientist - Coldplay

Dear J,

I forgive you. It's beautiful out here. You'd love it. Stevie says hi.

Amber

Day #13 driving through Utah (Arches National Forest)

DECEMBER 29, 2018

We Found Each Other in the Dark - City and Colour

Dear Future Husband,

I don't know who you are or where you are, but I like to think that I'm getting closer to you with each day that passes. The road to get to you feels long and never ending but it's been a beautiful one as well. I have some battle wounds, but I'm working on them as we speak, and pretty soon they will just be scars.

Some people close to me joke that I'm too wild to settle down but I imagine you will be just wild enough to keep up with me!

I hope you love Stevie as much as I do. She's my whole world right now but she could use a dad too. She's a great best friend for me but I can't wait to have a human best friend to watch her grow up with me. Some of the things she does are so funny! Plus it will be nice to have another travel buddy to join us on the road. It's hard putting up a tent and keeping Stevie from jumping all over it at the same time!

Sometimes I worry that I may never find you, but I refuse to give up hope. I know you're out there somewhere in this great big beautiful world.

I hope Stevie and I find you sooner than later.

Your future wife (and puppy)

Night #13 - White House Inn - Room 21, Sedona, Arizona

DECEMBER 30, 2018

Powerful - Major Lazer and Ellie Goulding

Dear Sedona,

You are magical! I have to be honest though, at first I thought everyone here was part of some weird cult. All the old people are hippies, everyone knew each other's names and there's a Reiki healer on every corner. It freaked me out! But then I walked to the Crystal Magic store next to my motel and while I was walking around the shop looking for souvenirs all of a sudden I had this overwhelming urge to cry.

I know you are well known for spiritual healing and there are several 'vortexes' around town but something in the middle of that rock shop hit me like a ton of bricks. I don't know if it was the crystals, the Arizona air or just exhaustion from the past two weeks, but I believe in the magic of you now! Thank you for leaving a little piece of you on my soul during this trip.

Amber

Day #14 - Hiked Bell Rock in the morning and started driving south

DECEMBER 30, 2018

Never Forget You - Zara Larsson, MNEK

Dear Jordan,

I was such a shitty girlfriend to you! I kept thinking about that when I was in Sedona today. I made a detour to the Chapel of the Holy Cross because I remembered you telling me about your parents taking you there when you were a kid. It was just as beautiful as I remember you describing it.

Despite utterly failing at trying to date you, I think you were my best friend in Chicago. It amazes me that you took care of me during my surgery even after we broke up. We literally went through every phase two people can. From co-workers to friends to dating to being exes and back to friends again. I'm sorry I was so terrible at the girlfriend part. At that point in time, I wasn't really ready for love, even though I loved you so much. You were the first person I ever dated who saw me the same way I saw myself.

I know we haven't talked a lot lately but I do miss the shit out of you and you'll always be an important person in my life. I always laugh so much every time I'm around you.

Thank you for being you and for all of the life lessons I've learned from you.

Until next time,

Amber

Night #14- Apache Junction KOA - Tent site T

DECEMBER 30, 2018

RIP 2 My Youth - The Neighborhood

Dear Chris and Dillon,

I miss you, little brothers! I know we've had our ups and downs but you're still my two buds.

You don't know this, but I talked to my therapist a lot about you two over the past two years. I have always felt so terrible that you two grew up with mom in the middle of her drug addiction while I got to live with Meemaw and Peepaw and miss out on a lot of the awful things you two had to endure as kids. She told me that I have survivors guilt and I have to look at life this way: it's almost like a person who has passed away would want me to live my best life and not sit and grieve over them forever. I have to pull myself out of my sadness and live life to the fullest because you'd still want me to be happy.

See, I never understood as a kid why I couldn't be with my mom and my brothers. I always wanted to be around you guys during the holidays and I always felt jealous because you two got to spend time with mom and I couldn't. I felt left out of some kind of special bond the three of you had. Then when life got hard for you two and you started having legal troubles I got so mad at mom and blamed her for never giving you two a chance at a better life.

Some people will see your past and think you are two guys who don't deserve a chance, but I look at you two as the little kids who were never given a chance. I know you both have huge hearts and I think part of you have been searching for the same thing I've been looking for.

I won't lecture you guys for the millionth time but I will say this... life is *so* good out here! There's so much more in the world than you have seen. There *are* good people who are full of love and kindness. Life will not always be fair so you have to be kind to yourself when you can. You two have such great passion and talent that should be shared with the world. It will get better if you let it.

I believe in you both. We can break the cycle that we were all born into. It's great out here and I hope you can come out here soon and find some of the same peace I'm starting to find.

Love,

Amber

DECEMBER 31, 2018

Little Wanderer - Death Cab for Cutie

Dear Traveling Brothers at the KOA in Apache Junction,

Thank you for the tips on apps to find campgrounds while Stevie and I travel! I downloaded them this morning. Also, thank you for the encouragement on camping getting better the further west I go after I told you the Mississippi story! Some times this trip can seem a little discouraging so I needed to hear your words of positivity!

Stevie had fun playing with your dog in the park and I'm grateful she had a playmate to wear her out! Don't worry, we stayed warm last night in the tent, Stevie cuddled me and I covered us both in hand warmers!

I hope you both have safe travels and a happy New Year! Also, thank you for telling me about the bad weather at the Grand Canyon! If you hadn't I'd probably be on my way there now and get stuck in the snow storm. I'm going to stick further south and find someplace warmer to go instead.

Sincerely,

The only person tent camping in the park

Day #15 - Driving some place warmer

DECEMBER 31, 2018

The New Year - Death Cab for Cutie

Dear Aunt Donna and Uncle Barry,

Thank you so much for letting Stevie and I come to stay the night tonight. The truth is I realized that I've skipped the holidays this year (which are normally my absolute favorite time of the year) and I honestly didn't want to be alone on New Year's Eve. It meant the world to me that you took the time to make a vegetarian meal for my arrival and were so kind to me when I arrived. I often think about how kind the two of you are even in the hard times and I look up to you both as examples of the kind of adult I want to be.

It's funny thinking about my past New Year's Eves over the years. There was 2000 when I stayed at Angie's and we waited in her basement for the world to end. (It didn't) There was 2005 where my then fiancé agreed that would be the year that we got married. (We never did) There was 2011 where my night ended with me kissing a semi-famous musician. (We never spoke again) There was 2012 where my boyfriend found me onstage doing the countdown in front of thousands of people and we got to have our kiss at midnight. (We broke up a year later) The rest is kind of a blur. It's funny how we put so much pressure on this one night to represent a better future for ourselves and to let go of all the bad things from our past. I'm realizing now that we can't erase the terrible things that happened to us, but we can embrace them and realize that even the hard times helped us get to where we are today.

I thought this year I would be at the Grand Canyon with Stevie watching the first sunrise of 2019 but a huge snowstorm stopped us from going there and to be honest I'm happier here and with people that I know and love. Plus it feels really nice to sleep in an actual bed for a change. I might not even make it to midnight it's so comfy here. Here's to my first adult stay in and not partying on New Year's Eve in as long as I can remember!

I love you both and I appreciate you so much.

Amber
Night #15, Lake Havasu City

JANUARY 1, 2019

Waking up the Giants - Grizfolk

Dear lady who walked over and loaned me a camp chair for the night,

THANK YOU!

I was so hesitant to take it from you at first but now I'm so glad I did. I'm sitting by the campfire looking at the Milky Way's edge (thanks to old man Gary from 2 RVs down for walking over and explaining to me what I was looking at) and all the other stars I could never see before.

You see it's very rare in life that I have those moments where everything feels right with the world and I am in pure bliss. Almost like I'm living in a movie. But right now is one of those moments.

2018 was a particularly bad year for me. I lost a pregnancy I didn't want to give up, had a major tumor removed from my uterus and thought I'd never be able to have kids, had my heart completely broken by the first person I had been able to fall in love with in a really long time and felt like I hit a brick wall with a career that had been my whole identity for as long as I can remember.

I had really started to think that this was it, I've hit my peak of all the happiness I was allowed to experience in my lifetime and now I'm just going to have heartache from now on. I was actually starting to accept all the bad things that were going to keep happening because I've already lived a life of a million dreams with my last job. I've met so many of my idols, gotten to work in the music industry which was always my dream, hell, I even had a billboard with my face on it in one of the biggest cities in the country. I've had everything I've ever wanted so why not let everything go downhill from now?

But then you brought me this damn chair.... and I'm sitting here looking at the Milky Way's edge...and all the stars in the sky that I've never been able to see before. Stevie is curled up in the tent and I'm by the warmest campfire from wood another camper left behind. I'm on the side of the bluest river you've ever seen and staring at a beautiful red mountain on the other side of the water.

If anyone has ever wondered if there's a heaven on earth, I think this is it.
Anyway, thank you for loaning me the chair for the night. I haven't felt this good in a long time.

Amber

Amber Cole

Night #16 - Buckskin Mountain State Park, Arizona - Tent site #79

114

JANUARY 2, 2019

Dear Old Man Gary from 2 RVs down,

Thanks for walking over this morning and asking me why I don't have a boyfriend doing this trip with me which turned into me awkwardly crying over coffee to a complete stranger about my love life.

I know it freaked you out, don't worry it freaked me out too.

It's not your fault you didn't know that I'm out here trying to heal a broken heart.

Don't worry, Stevie is a good sidekick though.

Alabama

Day #17 - Spending the day at Buckskin Mountain State Park

Amber Cole

hiking with Stevie

JANUARY 2, 2019

Sweet Surrender - Sarah McLachlan

Dear Buckskin Mountain State Park,

Staying here last night and tonight has been really special. There was an older man Gary who stopped by my campsite last night with his special green laser pointer. He drew patterns on the mountain across the way, then shined the bright green light into the river to expose all the fish swimming around at night and started pointing out all of the constellations in the sky with it. I actually think he was worried that I was out here alone in a tent in the middle of winter and just wanted to keep me company for a little while.

It was awesome to know that all the other people in RVs around here were looking out for me while camping on one of the coldest nights of the year. I think they all felt sorry for me really. From the lady bringing me a camp chair to use by the fire or the old man with an Australian accent who tried to loan me a fire starter after watching me struggle to get my first fire of the night started to all the other couples who would stop by my tent and ask me my story.

It was cool to hear everyone around the park call me Alabama. Everyone kept asking me what I dd for a living in Chicago which ultimately led to me telling them how to find my radio name. So then all the old couples kept saying things to me like, "Good luck Alabama!" or "Where to next Alabama?" or "Stay safe Alabama!"

I thought I would leave 'Alabama' behind when I did this trip and try to go find out who Amber is, but truth be told I actually miss being Alabama a little bit. It's a strange thing having two separate identities. One part of me is an entertainer sharing my whole life for the world to see and the other part of me is a complete shy introvert. It's almost like I'm two sisters in one body. I didn't realize that 'Alabama' and 'Amber' can both exist together until now. I keep trying to separate the two versions of myself when in all reality they both makeup who I am. It's okay to be contradictions of yourself sometimes.

Anyway, You have a great community here and staying here has opened up my eyes to a lot this past few days.

Thank you,

Alabama (The only tent camper on the river and yes I froze my ass off last night)

Night #17 - Buckskin Mountain State Park for another night

JANUARY 3, 2019

Sorry - Halsey

Dear Nanny,

I am so sorry that you are experiencing what you are right now. I know you are 92 with dementia so part of this is to help you, but how scary it must be for you right now to be taken away from your home one day and into a psych ward with a bunch of strangers. I know that you don't like being around a bunch of other old people!

I know the last few times I visited you, you couldn't remember my name but I know you knew me. You knew you loved me anyway and that is all that matters. You were really my best friend when I was a kid. Every day staying with you after school and how you'd bring my kitten to the elementary school when you'd pick me up. All the other kids loved walking over to your car to see my kitten!

Even now that I'm 33 years old you still have the spare bedroom in your house just how it was when we made it 'my' room as a kid. My first box of crayons and happy meal toys from the '80s are still right there! You held on to all of those things for me as an adult when no one else in my life even cared about those things. It's ironic that you had the forethought to save all these things for me so that I could remember my past when now it is your memory that is fading.

Most people will never know what it's like to have a great grandmother, but if it's anything like our bond it is such a special thing. You were like having a cool grandmother times 100! You did so many things to spoil me. You were wild as hell and I think I got that from you. A lot of people in our family say you are mean but I 'get' you and it's not mean, you just don't put up with people's bullshit. I admire that about you. You'd help anyone if you could.

You have been a great best friend to me growing up and I wish I were there with you right now to keep you from being scared. You took care of me when no one else would and I feel like I should come do the same for you. You loved me purely when everyone else in my life abandoned me and I appreciate you so much for that.

Thank you, Nanny, for helping to raise me.

I hope I will be half the woman that you were in my lifetime.

Love,

Amber

Night #18, Oasis Hotel, Las Vegas, Nevada Room #238

JANUARY 4, 2019

Every Other Freckle - Alt - J

Dear Las Vegas,

You were so good and so bad for my soul! It was nice to get out of a tent for a while and sleep in a hotel but the lights and sounds of the casino are so distracting.

People (Me) get sucked in by the dream of a better future here. If you just get one good spin on a slot machine it can change your whole life! I told myself I wouldn't gamble but after staying a second night I finally gave in to all of the flashing lights. I told myself I'd only allow myself to gamble with $200. Oh, how I should have stopped when I won $400!

I went to the Buffalo machine because that's the same one I went to when J and I were dating last summer and won some money. I picked Buffalo because he kept saying Buffalo was his animal and it was kismet that I had Buffalo skulls in my house so I figured it would bring some sort of luck. When he and I were still together it did bring me good luck! This time it started to. I hit a jackpot win and the wheel kept spinning and jumping from $100 to $200 to $400 and it wasn't long before a huge crowd was gathered around me at this damn slot machine watching my winnings keep growing!

But I did what most humans do and I got cocky. I tried to win more then ended up losing it all and spending another $200 trying to win my money back. It hurt my soul in the morning because I have no job and only a little bit of savings to my name and I really needed that money to survive. I guess its time to cash out my 401K so I don't have to worry about going completely broke before I find a way to work again.

At least I learned a lesson... Get out while the going is still good! Well at least appreciate what you have while you have it because before you know it you can lose it all. When we get cocky and think we deserve more is when we lose everything we have. Thank you for reminding me that I need to get back out into the woods with my tent! It was fun but I hope I don't come back and do this again!

Amber

Night # 19 - Oasis Hotel for a 2nd night in a row- Las Vegas Nevada

JANUARY 5, 2019

California Dreamin' - The Mamas & the Papas

Dear Sunset Inns in Victorville California,

Wow! I don't even know where to begin! The guy at the front desk is creepy and gave me hell for having Stevie (even though I told him she is a service dog and showed him her papers).

I wanted to come back in and ask for a refund but I didn't even feel like dealing with him again. I just couldn't stay at your hotel after walking into my room. It felt unsafe and then it looked like all the people coming into the motel were not the best neighbors for the night either. I took one walk in with Stevie and said, 'no way are we staying here.'

Had the weather been better we'd have stayed in the tent for the night, but the storms out here are unusually scary. The wind in

California feels like you're going to blow away with one big gust and I didn't want to risk setting up the tent in that mess.

Anyway if you thought the room was left unusually clean it's because we decided not to stay.

Thanks!

The girl who paid for room 17

Night #20, Econo Lodge, Hesperia California, Room #246

JANUARY 6, 2019

Mother (Don't Cry) - Ella Vos

Dear Mom,

I've been thinking about you a lot on this trip. I made it back to California where my life officially began. I see why you liked it so much here.

I got to meet my aunt Kathy on dad's side! She is more amazing than I could have ever imagined. She says hello. We talked a lot about your time with dad and she thinks that being with him is what broke you. I think the same thing too. All the stories I hear about you from before are of how great of a person you were and how everyone thought you were so much better than him.

I know you have a lot of guilt for the way everything happened when I was a kid and you became addicted to drugs. I want you to know I forgive you and I love you.

I wouldn't be the strong-willed woman I am today if my life had been any different. I know I've said some hurtful things to you growing up and I'm sorry. Now that I look back I realize that you were just a 21 year old with a kid and an abusive husband trying to do the best you could. I honestly don't know how you did it for as long as you did. I know you love me and I know deep down you have a huge heart. I like to think I get my big heart and sense of humor from you.

I know I've said, 'You're not my mom' so many times as an angry teenager but you are my mom and I love you so much! I hope one day you can find peace with yourself and let go of the demons you've been battling with for so long. The sunsets are so beautiful here and the whales swimming by are even more amazing! I wish you could be with Stevie and me to see it.

I love you.

Amber
Night #21 Crystal Cove State Park, California Campsite #59

JANUARY 6, 2019

I will Remember You - Sarah McLachlan

Dear Nanny,

I'm still thinking about you. This picture was taken the day you got admitted to the hospital.

I keep thinking about how a few years ago you gave me a book we made when I was a kid of clippings from old magazines of pictures that I liked. You kept that my whole life just to give back to me as an adult and I cried my eyes out when you gave it to me. You kept trying to give me all these things from my childhood that you still had and I wouldn't accept them because I didn't want to believe the fact that you might not be here much longer. Now that I'm looking back you knew what was happening and you just wanted me to have those memories of us before you would lose them.

One day I will write a book about you and all the funny things you did in your younger years. Stories about you are my favorite ones to tell. You don't know what I'm doing right now but I know you'd be proud because you were always a wild stubborn woman just like me!

Nanny, I love you and I'm going to miss you so much when you are gone but what's worse is that I already miss you while you're still here. I promise I'll be home to see you soon. Don't feel bad if you can't remember my name, I'll remember for the both of us.

Love,

Amber

Night #21 - Still at Crystal Cove State Park

JANUARY 7, 2019

Sober Up - AJR

Dear Hanna,

This journey I'm on keeps reminding me of the road trip we did two summers ago! I wish you were here with me. I'm not really sure if I ever told you why I took you on that trip, but I'll tell you now. I wanted you to go into your senior year of high school knowing that the world is so much bigger than the town we grew up in. I had never seen a world outside of Alabama until I was 21, packed my bags, and moved to California. That drive alone was such an eye-opener. I was almost mad that I had no idea such a world existed before then. Why had no one showed me how amazing this world was before now? That cross coun-try drive changed me and how I looked at life and I hoped that it would do the same for you.

Amber Cole

I didn't want you to miss out on all of the beauty the world has to offer, but here's the caveat, I don't want the world to miss out on all you have to offer either. You are so funny, talented, and have such a big heart. I know you're only starting college and just starting to figure life out and that's okay. I'm still figuring life out at 33 if I'm being honest. But what you should know about life as you get older is that it is short and the saying, 'You only regret the things you didn't do' is so true.

Your path won't be the same as mine but if you feel something in your heart please follow it. Never let anyone tell you that you can't be who you want to be. Never let anyone make you think you aren't good enough. Never believe a dream is too impossible to accomplish. You are such a special kid! (okay adult but I refuse to say it out loud). I've met a lot of people in my life but no one like you.

I know you will do big things and I'm so proud of the woman that you are becoming. Thank you for being my best friend and the little sister that I never had.

I love you,

Amber

Night #22 - Crystal Cove State Park, California, site #59

JANUARY 7, 2019

Meadows - Wild Child

Dear J,

Sometimes on this trip, I'm so sure that I'm over you but then I get a quiet moment on a beach in the middle of nowhere to sit and think, then you inevitably pop into my mind.

Usually, it's me going over every little detail of our relationship trying to figure out if what we had was real or if I just imagined we were more in my head. Tonight was different though. I thought about how excited we'd get when I was flying to Alabama to see you, or you were flying to Chicago to see me. You'd start counting down how many sleeps we had until we'd finally get to see each other. (I heard a woman at the grocery store telling her kids how many sleeps they had until the weekend today and it ripped my heart open because you are the only other person I've heard do that). And when we'd meet up I could see by the look in your face that you were genuinely happy to see me. Like the time I finally made it to Alabama after missing my first flight one weekend and you had a huge grin on your face and just picked me up and hugged me for what felt like an hour. I had never felt more loved or missed than those little moments with you.

I know you've been torn for a while now about love, life, and everything else. I know what it is like to imagine what life will be like if you chose one thing over the other and no matter what you chose you'll always wonder what could have been with the thing you chose to walk away from. Sometimes two really great choices can be so paralyzing. I've felt the same way about other choices in my life, so there is a part of me that understands.

This isn't one of those letters where I'm going to ask you to come back to me. You made a choice and I'm not going to try to change that. But I do miss you tonight and I know that you would love it here.

Don't worry about me or be sad about letting me go. I have Stevie and we will be fine. I know one day I'll find someone who will love me and look at me the same way you used to... genuinely happy to see me. I'll stop thinking about you in the quiet moments and think about how lucky I am to have found the life I was meant to live. I will be happy. Maybe this is a goodbye letter, who knows? You'll always be important to me. I'll always love you as a friend even though we didn't work out. It sounds crazy but you've always meant more to me than this romance. The true tragedy would be completely losing you from my life for good after knowing each other our whole lives. But I need to move on from you right now for my own sanity.

Thank you for all of the life lessons that you've taught me.

Amber

JANUARY 8, 2019

Low Life - X Ambassadors

Dear Stevie,

I don't think I've given you enough credit for being such a good road warrior. When I planned this trip, I thought, "She'll be fine, it'll be a fun adventure for both of us." Oh, how naive I was!

My car is jam-packed, so you have just enough space to lay with your butt in the back seat and your head up front with me. I can tell when you lay your head on my shoulder that you are sick of being in the car. You have an ear infection so I know you are uncomfortable on top of me trying to sneak these weird drops in your ears when you fall asleep. We've had some really cold nights where we had to share body heat to survive. You don't have a comfy couch to sleep on any more while I sit and watch

TV. You lost our walks down Lake Shore Drive to the dog park and you don't really understand what's going on.

I had no that not only was I uprooting my life, but I was uprooting your life too. You've been a lifesaver letting me wake you up in the middle of the night to go to the bathroom with me so I don't get scared. I know I get frustrated when you bark at everything but honestly, I'm grateful when you bark at night because you warn me of potential danger and scare off the people I don't want coming around our campsite.

You wake me up early enough to see the sunrise, even if I don't want to some mornings it's always worth it. You make me talk to people I otherwise wouldn't have when you run up to them for belly rubs. You're a great ear when I need to talk about something that's bothering me. I even think we have our own language with each other sometimes. I promise wherever my next job ends up being I will get a big yard for you to run around in and a bed so you don't have to snuggle in my one person sleeping bag. Thank you for being such a good dog. I'm sorry I'm not a better mom to you sometimes.

Love,

Mom

Night #23, Crystal cove State Park, site #46

PS. I know it was weird this morning watching me carry a fully set up tent to the other end of the park but they made us change sites since the one we were in was reserved for tonight.... but I know it beats driving to somewhere new!

JANUARY 9, 2019

Welcome Home, Son - Radical Face

Dear Matty,

THANK YOU for dragging me into the Los Angeles offices today. When you first told me to meet you there I thought, 'I'm not ready to talk to radio people or even think about going back to work yet,' but then I walked in and instantly felt like I had come back home.

Hearing you talk me up to people and then popping my head into John's office gave me back the confidence I needed. When I left my job in Chicago I was so certain that I was going to leave radio for good. I felt like I had done all I could do in this career and dedicated so much of my life to this. I felt like no matter how hard I tried I just couldn't be seen as the personality that I thought I was and get the break I had been trying so hard to get. I was starting to think that I just wasn't good enough and that I didn't belong in this business anymore. It's almost like going through a heartbreak and thinking you will never love again. I thought I would never be able to speak again.

You helped me get my voice back.

What I realized today is that I really do love radio and I'm good at it. Being able to walk into a radio station all the way across the country and to be known by other professionals in our industry reminded me of 23-year-old me who used to dream of being on a top 40 station in LA ten years ago. Thank you for that.

I didn't know that yesterday would actually be my last day on this trip but I cannot think of a more perfect ending. This whole time I've been trying to find my purpose and you helped me remember that I belong here and you inspired me not to give up. I appreciate you more than you know.

Alabama

Day #24 - Crystal Cove State Park for a few more hours before driving back to Alabama

Alcatraz - Oliver Riot

Dear Anthony,

Thank you for suggesting Crystal Cove State Park! That place is so incredible. I was crying this morning taking down my campsite because I honestly did not want to leave. If it wasn't for my great grandmother's health I'd have stayed another few days and kept on with my adventure.

Meeting you and Stacy was so impactful for me because until now I hadn't gotten to really spend any time with someone my age doing what I've been doing this past month. What was even more inspiring is that you've made traveling your life full time! That's a dream I hope to accomplish for myself one day. Talking to you about life on the road confirmed that I am doing the right thing for myself right now.

What most people don't realize is the world is so much bigger than their back yard. Traveling and seeing the sunrise on the mountains, the sunset over the Pacific Ocean, or a whale swimming past your campsite while having a cup of coffee can be life-changing. It was a million different tiny moments like those during this trip that slowly brought me back to myself.

Then talking to you about my future projects and seeing your excitement about my ideas made me realize I actually do have good ideas and gave me the courage to actually start using my creativity for something bigger than myself. Thank you for that! You were just the inspiration that I needed, and now I'm sad that the time we spent getting to know each other was so short.

As you said, it's never goodbye. I'll be back on the road again soon, so until our paths cross again! Have fun out there for me.

Amber / Bama

Night #24 - Microhotel - Wellton, Arizona

JANUARY 12, 2019

Running Just Incase - Miranda Lambert

Dear Miranda Lambert,

You don't really know me… we've met a few times when you were in Chicago and I interviewed you, but what you really don't know is that you've changed my life.

You see the last time you were in Chicago with Little Big Town you also had a booth for your animal rescue, Muttnation. I asked them if they needed fosters and a week later I picked up this hyper little German Shepherd mix puppy to keep for a few weeks. I didn't know that day that I would end up adopting this little wild child, but two weeks later I did.

Around the time I got Stevie, I was broken. I ended up leaving my job as a big radio personality on one of the biggest country stations in America. I packed my car with just the necessities, a tent, and my dog. I drove all over the country in a haze with Stevie trying to fix my broken heart.

What actually ended up happening was Stevie was the one who healed me. She cuddled me on cold nights to keep me warm. She made me laugh every time she'd jump on top of a picnic table or try to use a log of firewood as a chew toy when really all I wanted to do was sit and cry. She introduced me to strangers with her loving personality when I was too hurt to try to make friends with anyone. She made me realize that one day I will be a good mom even though I'm not sure if I'll ever be ready. She was my guiding light to freedom when I felt like I was getting lost in a dark tunnel of sadness.

Her name was Angel before I changed it to Stevie Nicks, but now that I'm looking back Angel was such an appropriate term for her.

So it was bittersweet when I saw a billboard on my way back to Alabama for your store, The Pink Pistol. I couldn't just drive by without taking my pup there to see the reason she and I are together now.

Like I said, you don't really know me but I needed to say Thank you. Thank you for rescuing so many animals with your charity Muttnation. Thank you for bringing these pups to their new and forever homes and Thank you for bringing Stevie and me together. You changed our lives.

Alabama

Day #27 - Last day on the road to Alabama in Lindale Texas

JANUARY 12, 2019

Drink a Beer - Luke Bryan

Dear girl who bought me a beer tonight,

You don't realize how much that beer meant to me. I know you got it because you liked my dog and were thanking me for letting you pet her, but what you don't know is that we had been in the car for four long days driving here from California. We came back to Alabama tonight because my great grandmother is dying.

I had been racing time to make it home before she passes so that I can tell her I love her one last time. I drove straight to her room in hospice before going anywhere else. Stevie waited patiently in the car and my Nanny was sleeping comfortably. I didn't even recognize my favorite woman in the world. The sassy outspoken woman I saw a month ago became this frail old lady overnight. It was the hardest thing I've ever seen.

She didn't wake up when I came in and I'm not sure she'll wake up at all. The doctors said she was awake and talking to everyone yesterday but I think I missed my chance to tell her goodbye. I sat with her for a few hours before kissing her on the head to tell her I loved her and go check into my hotel room to let Stevie stretch her legs.

Sitting in that hotel room trying to process what was happening was too much for me so I grabbed my dog and drove to The Nick for a beer. I wanted to just sit and try to remember Nanny the way she was when I was growing up: unapologetically outspoken, funny, and full of life.

Nanny has lived such a full life at 92 years old, and she's been ready to go for a while now, but I still don't think the rest of us that will be left behind are really prepared for this. I don't know if anything can really prepare you for the end of someone so important. All the things that had seemed so big just a week ago seem so insignificant now. At the end of the day, the people who shaped us need to know that they are leaving the world a better place because they were in it.

All the cliche's I've heard feel too real right now. Life is too short, time passes by so quickly and before we know it we are gone. If I'd had known the last time I saw Nanny might actually be the last time I get to speak to her, I'd have told her that my life was so much better because she was in it. I'd have told her that I can't imagine a life or a world without her in it. I'd tell her, 'Thank you for loving me and being my person when no one else was.'

Stevie doesn't understand all of this and I'm kind of in a haze right now. She's hated the past few days in the car so a scratch on the belly from you meant the world to her and the beer you bought me meant the world to me. That beer was so much more than you know.

Thank you for that.

Cheers,

Amber

JANUARY 13, 2019

Thank You For Today - Death Cab For Cutie

Dear J,

Nanny is dying and all I can think about is the time you went to cut her grass while we were dating. My grandparents paid you and you tried to give them the money back because you said it was too much. You told me that cutting her grass wasn't about the money… it was because I care about Nanny and you wanted to do it because you cared about me.

I fell so much more in love with you that day than I ever thought I would.

I took you to meet her last summer because she always asks me if I have a boyfriend. She was so afraid that I'd never find the love of my life and I think she didn't want me to be alone in the end. I knew I was in love with you when I took you to meet her and I wanted her to see that I'd be okay.

Of course, she freaked you out when she asked you if you were going to marry me the first damn time she met you! That is just Nanny. To the point, no bullshit. Ha! I guess she was right when you stuttered and she looked at me and said, 'He's not going to, you better find a better man!'

I think better isn't the right word, because you were always the right one for me in my eyes. But she still knew our fate when I was too blind with love to see it myself.

I don't know if you and I will ever see each other again but thank you for being kind to Nanny when we were together. It meant the world to me.

I see you.

Amber

JANUARY 15, 2019

Rivers and Roads - The Head and the Heart

Dear Nanny,

You passed away tonight. I don't even feel like this is real. I was fighting the time to get back to you and was so heartbroken when I realized that you weren't going to wake up so that I could tell you how much I loved you before you were gone.

Time on the road seemed to go by so slow, but then sitting with you the past few days time went by too fast. We all sat with you quietly not looking at our phones, not saying a word, and before we knew it hours had passed.

I still spoke to you several times the past few days and I hope you could hear me telling you it would be alright in your final moments. I'm so sorry that I wasn't around more when you kept asking me to come home and see you. I stayed with you tonight though because I wanted you to know that you wouldn't be alone when you passed.

You are so loved by so many people and I can't find words elegant enough right now to express how important you are to me and the rest of your family. I will never ever forget the big impression you have made on my life and left on my heart.

I love you more than words.

Amber

JANUARY 16, 2019

Folsom Prison Blues - Johnny Cash

Dear Chris,

Nanny died last night. I'm so sorry to be the one to break the news to you while you are in prison. I know you loved her so much and she loved you too.

Even though she'd always fuss about what you need to do to get your life straight! Ha! Every time I talked to her on the phone she'd always ask if I had talked to you. Nanny loved us unconditionally, faults and all.

I know it was hard to hear the news. When you told me you feel like life just keeps happening and you can't be a part of it I felt so bad for you being stuck in jail right now. I hate that this is a lesson for you but I really hope that it sticks. You have such a big heart and wonderful personality that just never had a real chance at a good life. The rest of us out here living have missed you for a long time.

You'll be out soon enough and I'll be here waiting for you to join this so-called thing we say is life. In the end, it will all be okay!

I love you and miss you so much,

Your big sister

JANUARY 17, 2019

Body in a Box - City and Colour

Dear Nanny,

Your funeral was today. It was the strangest thing I've ever experienced. I forgot you bought the burial plot next to you for me when I was a kid. So I got to see where I will be buried when my time comes. It will be an honor to lay to rest next to you.

It was strange seeing you in a casket. You didn't look like you. I hated it. Angie came in and kissed you on the forehead. She even spoke at the service. We laughed about how you told her to talk to her boobs and they would grow. (They never did!) I joked around with your brother Andy. I love him. He's so much like you. There were relatives I hadn't seen in over 10 years and some I didn't even recognize. Of course, my mom brought some drama to the funeral but did you expect any less of her? It wasn't too bad though. It was short and sweet and you'd have liked it.

We did a graveside service and whoever wanted to speak could. I had prepared something but left what I wrote down in the car. I was going to wait and read the room before speaking since I am just the great grandchild but when we all gathered around, Meemaw said anyone can speak if they want to, and everyone just looked at me. There was an awkward silence, and Meemaw said, 'Amber?'

In that moment I lost it. I almost forgot everything I wanted to say and I asked not to go first. It was silent so I said, 'Fine, I'll go.' Through tears and trying to catch my breath this is what I said:

"Nanny is a woman you will never forget. She's probably called every single one of us Asshole or Son of a Bitch at some point in our lives."

(Everyone laughed at that one.)

"But the greatest thing about Nanny is that she never lied. If she didn't like something you were doing or agree with something happening in your life she'd be the first to tell you. But she did that because she loved you and wanted what she thought was best for you."

"Nanny would also be the first person to do anything in the world for you. Like when I was five years old and my dad kidnapped me and took me back to California. Nanny was the one who rented the car and drove my mom across the country to bring me back to Alabama. I'm also sure that all of us have a similar story of Nanny's extraordinary kindness."

"The biggest life lesson that Nanny has taught me is that the people in our lives will do things we don't understand and they will even make us angry at times but we love them unconditionally and are there for them when it matters the most."

"Nanny left a huge impression on all of our hearts and I will never forget her. I love you, Nanny."

I know this is morbid but I've imagined before what I would say at your funeral when the time came and now that it has happened what I said was nothing like what I had imagined. Honestly, your funeral felt like a dream. I don't even think I was fully there. It was like I was having an out-of-body experience and watching it all happen in a movie. I hope I did you justice. That was the hardest speech I've ever had to do and I barely even made it through.

You're probably watching all of us with a wine cooler in one hand and your gun in the other just laughing at how silly we are all acting over your death. I hope that's what you're doing anyway. I know you are pain-free and surrounded by the people you love so much that you've lost in your lifetime.

I miss you so much, Nanny.

Amber

JANUARY 18, 2019

The Funeral - Band of Horses

Dear Evalee,

Thank you so much for the card you made me, and for setting that alongside a photo of Nanny in 'my room.' It was the sweetest thing to come home to when I got back from Nanny's funeral last night.

I've never met you until this week but I know your mom told you that I went to high school with her. I haven't talked to your mom much since we graduated but she was kind enough to open your home to me in my time of need.

Tonight she told me the story of how you made her take you to the store to do something nice for me after Nanny's funeral. She told me how you thought it was important to get a red frame for the photo of us and you picked a red bag of chocolates because chocolate makes you feel better. (It makes me feel better too!)

What you didn't know is that red birds were Nanny's favorite. She'd sit outside and whistle for a redbird to come to her and it would. We even buried her with a towel that she crocheted with a red bird on it. I went by Nanny's grave today and a red bag was floating in the air when I went by. Red keeps popping up and somehow you knew that the color red mattered.

I know you are only 6 years old but the words you wrote in my card were more impactful than anything I have read in a while. You and your mom have been lifesavers for me right now and I hope when you grow up you see how important this gesture was. Thank you for showing me kindness when I needed it. You are such a special kid.

Sincerely,

The girl temporarily living in your basement,

Miss Amber

JANUARY 19, 2019

All At Once - Pete Yorn

Dear Pete Yorn,

We've never met but somehow you've been a comfort for me in a lot of my worst times. I became a fan of yours in high school more years ago than I care to admit! 'For Nancy' was my feel-good anthem on my way to class in the morning. 'Lose You' was on repeat when I got into a terrible car accident and almost lost my best friend. 'Day I forgot' was the album my ex-fiancé and first love got for my birthday in 2004. I somehow swindled security to let me use the artist bathroom when I saw you performing at The Nick over 10 years ago. (Although it's not much better than the public bathrooms there!)

'Night Crawler' was the album that got me through my cross

country move from Alabama to California when I was 21, heartbroken and decided to leave all of my problems behind.

Somehow I find myself back in Birmingham, Alabama, thirteen years later, eating dinner with family after burying my great grandmother, and they mentioned that you were playing across the street. So I frantically looked for tickets to your sold-out show at Saturn and bought a pair.

I walked in when you started playing 'All At Once,' and it hit me like a punch in the gut. Nanny used to say all the time how she wanted to just burn her house down and that lyric seemed to bring everything that had happened in my life the past thirteen years full circle.

We run away from our home town to be someone bigger than we are, but we always end up right back where we started, missing who we were before we became adults. For a brief second watching you tonight brought me back to seventeen year old me, before one of the most important people to me had died, before I had been heartbroken by a boy, before I went out into the world and figured out that being a grown-up isn't as much as it's cracked up to be.

Anyway, you don't know me but your show tonight was just what my soul needed and it was kismet that you were here when I was. Thank you for writing such powerful songs and for still touring. I needed to hear your music tonight.

Sincerely,

Just another fan

JANUARY 27, 2019

Satellite Heart - Anya Marina

Dear Universe,

After taking some time off to travel and clear my head, I'm ready to come back and join the rest of the world.

See you soon,

Amber

JANUARY 30, 2019

. . . .

April - Nick Mulvey

Dear World,

I started this thinking that I needed to fix my heart. I was broken over a boy who left me, a job that felt wrong, and just all the other bullshit that comes with being a grown up. My life had become an overgrown forest that needed to be set on fire to burn away all of the weeds so that new trees could flourish.

The weeds growing in my life sprouted slowly over time, but they were beginning to suffocate me. Toxic relationships... fake friends... junk I had accumulated over the years and never used... the idea that money and fame were the keys to happiness... the false comfort of an overpriced apartment in downtown Chicago with a beautiful view that I took for granted after a week of living there.

I needed to burn all of those things down so that I could start fresh and get lost in the world. Leaving everything behind was the freest I've ever felt in my entire life. In losing everything I knew, I could finally begin to find my true self again.

I believe that we build our own personal prison by believing what other people say we are supposed to do. We build our 'happiness' around some invisible standard that society has created, and we make ourselves miserable trying to live up to that standard. In turn, we grow angry, sad, depressed and begin to act out against ourselves and against everyone else around us. And for what? We are really only acting out against the prison that we put ourself in. We are the only ones that hold the key to get out.

Life is too short to try to live up to something we aren't even sure of ourselves. Before you know it the people you love the most are gone then you got old and will die too. On your dying day can you look back at your life and answer these questions with absolute certainty that you are happy with the answer?

Did you take every chance you wanted to take? Were you kind to the people who crossed your path? Did you love with your whole heart? Were you happy when life was going well for you? Did you surround yourself with people who loved you for who you truly were? Were you present for all of the important moments? Did you truly live?

We only get one life on this earth and when you see the big picture, the day to day things we stress over are so insignificant. Tell the people you love how much they mean to you. Take a break from the world and spend time with your family. Marvel at nature. Take care of the planet. Be kind to a stranger. Even the tiniest gesture can change someone's life. And most of all, live your life for you. Do the things that nurture your heart and soul. Don't worry about what other people will think. The same people who will say you are crazy for doing something wild will be the people who envy your freedom from afar. Whatever you do in this life, be free.

Amber Cole

Made in the USA
San Bernardino, CA
09 June 2019